CALVIN COOLIDGE

Farmer — Mayor — Governor — President

HIS LIFE — ITS LESSON

THE CORNERSTONE

"Allured to brighter worlds, and led the way."

— Goldsmith.

THE MOTHER OF THE PRESIDENT

"About his cradle all was poor and mean save only the source of all great men, the love of a wonderful woman. When she faded away in his tender years, from her death bed in humble poverty she dowered her son with greatness. There can be no proper observance of a birthday which forgets the mother."

—Lincoln Day Proclamation — 1919 — C. C.

CALVIN COOLIDGE

His First Biography

From Cornerstone to Capstone
To the Accession

By R. M. WASHBURN

Author of "Smith's Barn"

BOSTON
SMALL, MAYNARD AND COMPANY
PUBLISHERS

Printed in the United States of America

THE MURRAY PRINTING COMPANY
CAMBRIDGE, MASS.
BOUND BY THE BOSTON BOOKBINDING COMPANY
CAMBRIDGE, MASS.

WITH AFFECTION

TO

CHARLES SUMNER BIRD

The Outstanding Political Layman in Massachusetts

The Secret

Silence — Uncommon Sense — Wit — Mystery

Fidelity — Preparation — Two Allies — Fate

*Omnia Praeter Strepitum et Clamorem**

* Everything except noise.—*Interpreted for outside of Boston.*

FATE

It was only a plain New England farm among the folks of the hills of Vermont. There was neither train nor telephone nor trolley. It was much as God had made it. There lay a child, young and weak and helpless, and a mother proud in the gift of prophecy. And there stood by the child's cradle one great and powerful, Fate. She had sought him out in his simple atmosphere. Her protecting arm she raised above him. She took him by the hand and ever led him on. She saw in him virtue to be recognized. Capacity was quick to see and to seize opportunity. She commissioned into the service a good and a great merchant of Boston. She cried gangway to a creditable public servant, who stood high and third on Beacon Hill, who blocked his progress, who was then drafted into the grand army of the politically dead. She commanded striking policemen to open a path before him. A great Police Commissioner gave wings to his feet. She led him towards horizons as boundless as the seas, fame, power and financial freedom. She set him in the seats of the mighty. Even Death rode on before him and cleared the way.

IN EXPIATION?

I HAVE known him for sixteen years, since we were in the House in Massachusetts in 1908. In 1913, when he was Senate-Chairman of the Committee on Railroads, I was House-Chairman. For five years we were legislative colleagues.

His First Biography is an attempt to write of a personal friend as he is. He has a marked individuality which appeals and stimulates an honest, human story; history and romance, fact and fancy. It seeks to cover the whole keyboard, setting out cheerfully into the happy notes of the treble and venturing at times among the gloomier notes of the bass. It ventures to touch upon his particular individualities, not only for the truth but also to lighten the portrait with amusement, it is thought innocent. It thus cinches its sincerity, sets off its praise. It analyzes honestly his success and its causes. It also attempts to respect the proprieties of the Presidency.

It drives at quality not quantity, symbolized by the man and by his characteristic caution to the Massachusetts Senate:

"Be Brief."

R. M. W.

236 Bay State Road,
Boston.
September 15, 1923.

CONTENTS

ILLUSTRATIONS

CALVIN COOLIDGE

CHAPTER I

CALVIN THE SILENT

"I have never been hurt by what I have not said."—C. C.

ON the fourth day of July, 1872, more than fifty-one years ago, in the columns of a news sheet, *The Blueberry*, which succeeded occasionally in making its appearance in the town of Plymouth, Vermont, appeared the laconic entry: "Born, to Victoria Josephine Moor and John Calvin Coolidge, a man-child, John Calvin Coolidge, Junior." These tidings of great joy did not cause banks to close or business to be tied up, for that was a country of farmers only, and those who read it were tillers of the soil and not seers. However, the little stranger, with a foresight sound and characteristic, had chosen as the day of his advent one which the neighbors were bound to celebrate.

The child, an auburn-haired, smooth-faced

3

babe with a proboscis somewhat attenuated, was
as unique as he lay in his cradle as he was to
be as a man. He seemed troubled. The atmosphere of ambition enshrouded him. He seemed
restless and anxious for change and for progress. The baubles which divert and stimulate
the prosaic young seemingly had no charm for
him, nor did anything which tender hearts or
wise heads could plan. He lay in his new bed
and cried and when he had tired of crying, he
wept and then he cried again. All this apparently with deliberation and for a purpose and
as a means to an end.

*For the first effort of the child and
the man has been always, not to play
but to think.*

A mother solicitous through unselfish love
sat by his side, intent upon bringing him peace;
and a father with the more selfish purpose of
sleep. The family physician bent over the crib
with that rural versatility which had familiar-
ized him with the whole gamut of bodily afflic-
tions, from rheumatics to melancholia. Noted
psychologists too were added to the throng, not
alone for the advancement of medical science

but with the hope of solving a problem which seemed to baffle all.

These all followed his infant gaze as it swept the plain walls of that Vermont farmhouse. They watched his eyes as they rested and became riveted upon the only decoration in that room, a portrait of that Great Liberator of the Dutch, of the low lands of Holland, a Prince and a Count of Nassau, William the Silent. And they gave it to the child.

Then peace came to that household and to its mother. The father slept. The general practitioner went his way and the noted specialists returned to the great centers. And the child studied the face and the features of the portrait and then, placing the end of one of his small fore-fingers upon the mouth of that great prince and the other upon one of his ears, he too was content and happy and he too slept, and peace overwhelmed that small house and that small family.

And those who sat about the child construed the lessons of what they had seen to be: first, that he would leave the hill country of his birth and also live close to his adopted meadow lands along the banks of the Connecticut; and second, that he fastened the hopes of the political success that was to be his upon the determination, not to talk but to listen, not upon the power of speech but upon the possibilities of silence. From that hour he then became and has since continued,

*Calvin the Silent.**

*Title originated by R. M. W. in a speech at Weeks Dinner, Boston City Club, November 8, 1917, when C. C. was Lieutenant-Governor.

CHAPTER II

AMONG THE HILLS

*"Vermont is my birthright. Here,
one gets close to nature, in the moun-
tains, in the brooks, the waters of
which hurry to the sea; in the lakes,
shining like silver in their green setting; fields tilled, not by machinery
but by the brain and hand of man.
My folks are happy and contented.
They belong to themselves, live within
their income, and fear
no man."—C. C.*

CALVIN COOLIDGE is proud of Vermont and
her nature, his folks and their simplicity. Their
praises he often sings. Otherwise, he seldom
praises things; or men, whether under obligation to them or not. Independent of praise himself, he cannot understand its sweet stimulus to
others. He knows the plain people. He thus
conserves their rights. He is one of them. It
has been said that God loves the plain people
most because he made so many of them. This

7

story of the boyhood of the President among the
hills of Vermont is a story of a faithful and
industrious son. This is all. This is much. He
has always led an orderly life, of preparation
for tomorrow, lest the grasshopper become a
burden. There is an old adage:

> *"The bee gains little from the flower,*
> *A stone a day will raise a tower,*
> *Yet the hive is filled, the tower is*
> *done*
> *If steadily the work goes on."*

The young are impatient of counsel from
those who have already walked the way. They
often insist upon burning their wings around
their own lamps. A young woman whom a
grandmother at an afternoon tea had ventured
to advise did not hesitate to say: "Grandmother,
you are wrong." Her grandmother then replied as she handed the child a buttered scone:
"Mary, if you were about to climb the Matterhorn and a guide should tell you that your shoes
should be cleated, would you say to him: 'You
are wrong.' He has climbed the Matterhorn.
So have I, for life is but a series of summits to
be sought." What man is there who would not

live his life again if he could and would cap-
italize his experience and that of others. What
mental agony like the realization of mistakes,
irreparable, where the nail holes always remain.
History gives each one of us a blank page, a
fresh and clean page to write his history upon.

Calvin Coolidge has lived with his ears and
his eyes wide open for counsel. He has always
been a student of history because he believes it
has a lesson for today and for tomorrow. His
mind is always open. Should he be a candidate
for the Presidency in 1924 against the great
motor-maker, the Phœnix of Detroit, the issue
may well be Ford's creed: "All history is bunk."
Boy and man, small and great, he has always
had purpose, and determination enough to carry
it out. He has always done not only the day's
work but he has done it during the hours of the
day. To him, the hours of the evening have
been hours for forward thinking and forward
planning. The young man is too much content
with his comfort of today. He is too apt not to
look beyond the dinner and the dance of tonight.
He forgets the day when perhaps a cloud of
storks may complicate his situation. Hence his
lot, easy today, is a struggle tomorrow. Cool-

idge then as now was never content simply to contemplate the small single stickers securely sheltered on the placid surface within the breakwater, but his glass has always been trained on the rough outside sea, where he was to set sail. Even today his crest is not the words: *Je suis arrivé.* Enough of philosophy. Theory is easy. Practice is hard. It is easy to write a recipe for the Presidency but hard to secure an election to the Legislature.

This is another story of The Log Cabin to The White House

It is true that our hero did not come from as far back as Lincoln. He has gone as far, however, for while he may not have been born in a log cabin it must not be forgotten that the civilization of his day has advanced. Relatively his termini have been as far apart.

John Calvin Coolidge, the father of the President, is a farmer at Plymouth, Vermont, as his ancestors have been before him. Plymouth, also known as "The Notch," is in Windsor County eleven miles north of Ludlow the nearest railroad center for the town, on the Boston and Maine Road. It is southeast from Rutland.

The family originally settled at Watertown in Massachusetts in 1630. John Calvin Coolidge, Senior, has earned the respect of the community, for he has sat in the State Legislature, House and Senate. He has also been Constable, Collector, Superintendent of Schools, Deputy Sheriff, Notary Public, Selectman and State Assessor. He has also served on the staff of former Governor W. W. Stickney. The quantity of these public trusts, which he has been unable to resist, no one holds public office willingly, may well be set off against the quality of the Presidency and have led the boy Cal to look upon the latter as a reasonable aspiration for a Coolidge. Of such has been his atmosphere.

When Cal was born his father kept the village store and he also shod horses and collected insurance premiums. There is little to be done that he has not done.

His father is a dirt farmer and not a so-called gentleman farmer, by which is meant, that the farm supports him and not he the farm.

It is a plain farm in its buildings. There never was a telephone upon it until August 3, 1923.

It was later removed. The hand of civilization has hesitated before it. There are many like it in Vermont. His father married, first, Victoria Josephine Moor, the mother of the President, who died March 14, 1885, when he was twelve years old. He later married Carrie G. Brown, who died in 1920, and who was as much of a mother to the boy in his maturer years as any step-mother could be. The only other child was a daughter, Abigail G. Coolidge, an own sister of Calvin Coolidge, who died March 6, 1890, at the age of fifteen.

John Calvin Coolidge, Junior, our hero, first met his father, July 4, 1872. He had not then formed his later faculty of fixing faces and names, even that of his father, a great asset in politics. It's sweet to hear one's name, even that of Jones. His name the boy wrote J. Calvin Coolidge until he located in Northampton, when he became simply Calvin Coolidge. With characteristic foresight Cal had planned to arrive in Plymouth independent of transportation facilities upon a national holiday, which the family began to recognize with a double propriety, of the strength of which they then had small appreciation. He was born in the

BIRTHPLACE. THE CILLEY STORE

Born in rear right-hand room, ground floor

rear right hand room, as one faces the house, of
what is now known as "The Cilley Store."   He
was a red-haired baby.

He is the first red-haired President of
the United States.

In his school days, he was known as "Red"
Coolidge.   In the plain atmosphere of his birth
and in the individuality which he early devel-
oped, he came to suggest Abraham Lincoln.   He
became known for his unique speech, that is,
when he spoke.   Calvin the Silent he was and
always has been.   When one says as little as he
says, it ought to be good.   The opportunity to
concentrate is great.

Calvin Coolidge was good raw material.   He
had an instinctive sense of right and character
enough to live it out.   His father says that he
was a good and industrious boy, that he never
had to tell him what to do for it was done. "He's
always been that and I guess he always will be.
He wasn't extraordinary.   He did his work at
school.   He was a great hand on the farm.   I
made no rules because then there's no chance to
break them."   His teachers unite today in the

testimony that he was a good student, quiet,

"kind of stately,"

dignified and not mischievous and that he kept
to himself. He was a faithful boy. He was
neither popular nor unpopular in the town, liked
or disliked. If the boy Cal ever looked upon
the hearts of the village maidens as citadels to
be taken, his campaigns must have been conducted cunningly, for there is no justification,
even of a suspicion. If they in their turn did
not seek unduly to annex the scion of the leading
house in the town, forgetting a maidenly modesty still indulged in by the old-fashioned, it
was because he had not confided in them his
accession to the Presidency, which Fate had decreed to him.

On one occasion, for some undetermined reason, having been found at a village dance, where
he had refrained from leading The Quadrille,
The Ladies Chain or indulging in The Portland
Fancy, his grandmother, who was one of the old
school, whatever that may mean, rewarded his
virtue with one dollar. Cal never made a dollar
more easily, for he and the jazz have always
been strangers. He has always been immune

from the frailties which assail human beings.

He has never been spanked, boy or
man, either by hand in the nursery
or by machinery at the polls.

One night his aunt was sleeping at the house.
She heard steps on the first floor. Fearing the
loss of the Coolidge crown jewels, she donned
the kimono kept hanging in all well-appointed
houses, opened the door and went downstairs
where she found little Cal. He explained that
he was filling the wood-bin, which he had forgotten. He declined to retire, in reply to her plea.
He would finish the job. He did. Calvin Coolidge never retires, he goes to bed. He is never
ill, sometimes sick. He was born, not in Boston,
but in Vermont.

One Sunday morning at church when the por-
tières had been drawn back and the choir un-
covered, pursuant to the practice of the times,
and the minister was well under way, little Cal
fell asleep, it must be confessed with some
shame. Then a small boy, behind, forthwith
plunged a forefinger into Cal's warm-hued hair,
which finger he then rested upon the pew-top
and proceeded to tump, after the manner of the

village smith. This caused much unholy mer-
riment in the congregation. Such homely hap-
penings as these have been harvested with some
difficulty, but with the hope of picturing the
human atmosphere in which our little plant was
nurtured. Cal first went to school in the little
red schoolhouse at Plymouth, the building now
having been succeeded by another.

He early took his place upon the farm. While
many of the boys of today are feverishly putting
on the golf green, Cal was happy in pursuing to
its lair the sportive potato. He early and always
has been an artist in the mowin', where he has
found physical strength, character and a pan-
ama hat vital. He early became an adept in
divorcing the lowing herd which winds slowly
o'er the lea from the raw material which makes
for butter and cheese. It is a rare distinction
which has come to the bovines of Plymouth, to
be milked by a President. He has always
adorned a hayrake with as much facility as a
reviewing stand.

In later years, a cloud-burst has broken upon
the people, portraits of Cal in smock frock and
cowhide boots, an inheritance from his grandfather, his grandfather's legislative attire. The

Bain

PORTRAIT OF A COW.* SMOCK FROCK AND COWHIDE BOOTS
1923

*Labelled pursuant to the practice of museums

sordid have been quick to suspect and have looked upon them as a costume which Cal assumes for effect upon the electorate.

These he wore when he was obscure.
These he wears when he is great.

According to the late Elihu Burritt: "It is as much the uniform of the English farmer laborer as is the red-coat that of the English soldier." These suspicious ones do not know Cal, for his essence is simplicity and sincerity. He is as much himself at work in smock-frock and boots as the sometimes effete children of Beacon Street, when they loll in dinner jackets, or decolleté and lapis lazuli.

His life became early a series of but two sensations, of work and recuperation for work. This habit has so fastened itself upon him that he has always gone home at vacation time to take his place upon the farm. He has never played, boy or man, marbles, baseball or anything, except for a fortnight's lapse at golf, when he was satisfied of the error of his way, repented, reformed, retired and denied. His only avocations have been the gratification of an almost instinctive philosophical sense with the best books, a love of nature which shows in his speeches, and the habit of walking.

Apparently he has ordered his life wisely.

He prepared for college, graduating in 1890 at Black River Academy in Ludlow. On his graduation he delivered an "Oration on History." Most of the orations in the country are delivered by the young in the tepid days of June, when "The boy stood on the burning deck," and "Horatius at the bridge" are common echoes. Although qualified for college at eighteen, Cal studied a year at the Academy at St. Johnsbury, also in his native state.

When he had exhausted the educational resources of the county, he said: "Father, do you want me to take my place on the farm?" There was no discussion at home, whether he should or should not go to college. His father has always been proud of his son; and silent, as all Coolidges and Vermonters. Fate had determined that the boy should go. He went. This is the whole story of the farm, of a faithful son, industrious at home and at school. It is not a long story because like the boy it is a story, not of quantity but of quality. The story of the boy is the story of the man, the whole story. It is a good deal of a story.

Cal he was. Cal he is.

CHAPTER III

Amherst '95

"TERRAS IRRADIENT"

For those some few of our readers who are happier perhaps in some patois rather than in lingua Latina these words, the Amherst motto, are interpreted to read: Thou shalt enlighten the earth. Surely Calvin Coolidge has already removed his light from under a bushel, for his Alma Mater.

September 20, 1891, stands high in the annals of the burg of Plymouth. Then father Coolidge hitched the old bay mare into the Tilbury to drive Cal to Ludlow to take the train for Amherst. It was an eventful day for the town and for Cal. The boy spread upon his cot bed his wardrobe preparatory to packing, with all the anxious care of one about to take his first journey from home. There was a full quota of linen of a type which could be inverted, known familiarly as reversible cuffs. A sampler not unknown in those days was last considerately folded and enclosed by him in

20

VACATIONS ON THE FARM

'91–'95

his reticule. Into this had been wrought words to read: "The Notch," in squares, each by the skilful and romantic hands of a maiden of the hamlet, who thus sought to protect for themselves his heart, immune from the wiles of the sirens at a seminary bearing the odd name of Smith and lying adjacent to the academic domains. Their little hearts would have rippled and they would have qualified for sanitariums could they have then known that Cal was about to take the road which led towards Lake Champlain and the house of Goodhue, by the way of his college town and his adopted city of Northampton. Worse than this he retains the sampler. That great epochmarker of John T. Wheelwright, Harvard '76, which blazed a trail in literature and shrivelled Dickens, known as "Rollo's Journey to Cambridge," looked upon by Cal as a sort of Baedeker, he carefully tucked inside his tunic. An "interlinear," to interpret foreign languages, was unknown in his library. At the last moment he delayed a somewhat impatient father long enough to run to the village store for a supply of "Wrigley's P. K. Chewing Sweet," enough to safely

carry* him through the fall term. His father
was later encouraged to look upon this as a
humanizing transition on the part of a boy who
had hitherto done few things like other boys.
Hence this homely incident is recited here for
their encouragement.

> *Then Plymouth had an Amherst man*
> *and Cal become great in the town,*

which now looks back with wonder and humili-
ation that it could have been so easily impressed.
In those days such a step as this was no small
distinction, when now it is not a matter for
notice. Then, it was a stake-buoy in the life
of father and son, for the boy was leaving
home for the valley of the Connecticut where
he was to study and to live. Cal left the smock-
frock hanging on a peg in the front entry at
home, touching evidence of his absence. The
cowhide boots stood in a corner of the barn
and Cal least feared that they would be pur-
loined for a village dance. There is strong
suspicion that the boy broke his usual rule of
taciturnity at the station long enough to inquire

* A deliberate and proud use of the only split infinitive
in Boston. Endorsed by C. C. To be noted and condoned by
the Hon. Robert Grant, Doctor of Letters, Harvard.

the fare to Amherst. This exception was perhaps justified.

Coolidge became a member of the class of 1895. He then as now was unassuming, he went his own way. He was silent. What he said, when if he said it, was good. When he had unpacked his portmanteau, which travellers carried in those days and had deposited it with the reticule in the closet, and had spread about his room the family photographs pursuant to the practice of the times, not forgetting a picture of the farm on the wall,

he began immediately a methodical order of life as has always been his wont.

He took no part in athletics. Hence he was not thus facilitated into the public notice. He never tackled low nor did he ever know the exhilaration of seeking to snare in the outer garden the elusive fly. He was not alive to the example of another Coolidge, William Henry, who had adorned for seven long years the pivotal bag at Cambridge. Only the disabilities of old age forced his retirement. Calvin might easily have trained down and qualified

for the crew, if there was one, could he have
delegated the obligation to urge it on, or, in the
vernacular, to coach it, which goes with that
office.

He made friends slowly. When they knew
him, they came. While he appeared cold on
the outside, they found him warm on the inside.
There was nothing about him to impress immediately any one. When he had acclimated
himself, however, and they on their part had got
used to him, they came to appreciate him, his
uncommon sense, his keen and terse wit and
comment on men and affairs. Sometimes in
a laughing group he would sit listening in
silence for a long time and then suddenly and
unexpectedly utter a monosyllable which would
convulse the house. He would come into the
room of a friend at eight in the evening, say,

"Hello, William," never Bill,

produce a book which he read until eleven and
then retire with a "Good-night, William." It
was a stimulating communion. In short he was
then as he is now, quality not quantity. He
never spoke unless he had something to say.
Often then he was silent. The country needs

more men like him, not men who can talk but
men who can listen and act, deeds, not words.

He was a faithful, good student, not brilliant or spectacular in any way, but what he
assimilated he held. The world's captains have
not always been its quick thinkers. Although
his father had always been able to support him
comfortably, Cal had none of the disabilities
of wealth and paid for his sustenance less than
two and one-half dollars a week. There was
no lower rate in the town, and a good rate even
in those days. He never could seek to qualify
for a cruise of the New York Yacht Club until
he came into the possession of *The Mayflower*
as President.

He was known in college as "Cooley." This
was suggested not only by his surname but
because when he sat with those who did not
know him well, they sought sanctuary in mittens
and mufflers and studied the methods of the
Eskimos for maintaining their circulations. As
they began to think they understood him, they
began to lay off their wraps. In his senior year at
college, there is a portrait of him extant when
he assumed a responsibility though only tem-
porarily, which only the Hon. Grafton Cushing

has safely carried in politics, he wore a stick.
More than this and worse than this, he wore
gloves, a white cravat and a chapeau which
seemed to yearn for Broadway.

> *Any one who can secure and will*
> *destroy this plate can have a seat*
> *in the Cabinet.*

This portrait was a distinct lapse for him. For
once and once only, Cal was not himself.

In the summer of 1892 on his return to
Plymouth with a full appreciation of the rank
of sophomore, which little can equal, he was
invited to deliver The Independence Day
Oration. It would have been a reflection on the
young man to have called it simply an address.
This distinction came naturally to him for he
could then speak more languages than any one
in the hamlet, or all combined. The old in-
habitants still talk of this day and this oration.
They say that Cal was profligate with all the
intellectual resources of the library at Amherst.
He walked upon the clouds. When he had
warmed up and struck his stride, he ventured
to emphasize the proposition: "The earth had
shook with the hurried retreat of the British

regulars from Concord and Lexington." To
the form of this allegation Calvin may not now
be loyal. In its substance the earth no more
than teetered then as set off against the magni-
tude of the Great War. The youth may have
imbibed too freely at the academic fount. For
once he played upon the passions of an audience. Under the power of his oratory, eyes
were dimmed, throats choked and brakemen
collapsed like anemic women.

That day Cal pulled out every stop.

From that day, the natives came to look for his
vacation summers on the farm with a certain
mingled dread and joy, for home he always
came, for with him work was an avocation.

In his junior year Coolidge entered into the
college debates where his clear perception of
issues made a marked impression. In that year
a local bard in *The Amherst Olio* emphasizes
the unhappy fact that for once Cal was asleep
at the switch, in these lines:

> "The class in Greek was going on;
>   Old Ty a lecture read —
> And in the row in front there shone
>   Fair Coolidge's golden head.

"His pate was bent upon the seat
  In front of him; his hair
Old Tyler's feeble gaze did meet,
  With fierce and ruddy glare.

"O'ercome by mystic sense of dread,
  Old Ty his talk did lull —
'Coolidge, I wish you'd raise your head,
  I can't talk through your skull!' "

In his senior year he entered a contest open to seniors in all American colleges and universities and won a first prize of one hundred dollars for an essay: "The Principles of the Revolutionary War." During the summer evenings his father had noticed him much at the table in the sitting room, with books and papers.

When he wanted the lamp, Cal had it.

He did not ask him what he was doing. Cal never told him. If he ever learned, it was undoubtedly through the columns of *The Blueberry*.

Coolidge was asked to deliver the Grove Oration, when he graduated. This was strong recognition of his wit. This oration takes its name because delivered in the college grove.

Coolidge was always modest. He never sought
a place in the sun. Hence he was very happy
in the shade of the grove. He graduated with
the degree of A.B., cum laude, or, for our
little readers, with praise. When in June,
1919, President Meiklejohn for the college gave
him the honorary degree of LL.D., he spoke of
his essence as

"adequate brevity."

There is a distinct propriety in recording
here an estimate of Calvin Coolidge by George
D. Olds, A.M., LL.D., Acting President of
Amherst College. "The Class of 1895 is a class
of which the college is peculiarly proud.
Among his classmates and contemporaries were
Dwight W. Morrow of J. P. Morgan and Com-
pany; Herbert L. Pratt, Vice-President of the
Standard Oil Company of New York; Lucius
R. Eastman of Hills Brothers; Professor Allen
Johnson of Yale; Cornelius J. Sullivan, a well
known New York lawyer; Frank D. Blodgett,
President of Adelphi College, Brooklyn; the
late Charles D. Norton, banker and financier;
George D. Pratt, who was a conservation com-
missioner under Governor Whitman; Edward W.

Capen, Dean of the Hartford Theological Seminary; Professor Eugene W. Lyman of the Union Theological Seminary; Harlan F. Stone, Dean of the Columbia Law School; Ex-Mayor Walter R. Stone of Syracuse; Professor Archibald L. Bouton of New York University; Howard Halligan, Vice-President of the Western Electric Company; Professor Frederic B. Loomis of Amherst; Roberts Walker, a former President of The Rock Island Railroad Company; Percy Deering, Coolidge's roommate, prominent since in the public life of Maine.

"Coolidge early revealed the characteristics which have made his personality so marked in public as well as private life. He was taciturn, reticent, epigrammatic in his way of speaking, with unusual poise for a first year man. Self-control and will power were evident in his every act. He was methodical in the extreme, always in his place yet never in haste.

He seemed always to have time to do the right thing, a man to whom an emergency was an opportunity.

He was not what is called a good mixer. Indeed it was in a way hard to know him in the

early days of his college life. He did not
join a college fraternity at the outset of his
course, but, when an upper class man, became
a charter member of the Amherst Chapter of
the Phi Gamma Delta Fraternity. His classmates did not wake up to the possibilities of
the man until late in his course when they suddenly became aware of his wisdom touched
with whimsical humor. At the close of his
course he won the distinction of being chosen
Grove Orator, the humorous speaker of Class
Day, and left the impression of having been
one of the best Grove Orators that Amherst had
known for years.

"There were few electives in Coolidge's day
and he enjoyed, shall we say, the advantages
of a rather rigid curriculum. The record shows
that he did good work in mathematics, English
and French. Unlike most of his college mates
he had the courage to carry his mathematics
through a second year. He was interested in
Greek and Latin, and it is a significant fact that
two of his important addresses since he entered
public life have been in advocacy of the classical curriculum. In the latter part of his
course there was some freedom of choice and

he became especially interested in debating,
philosophy, history, and political science.
Amherst was at the time a college containing
less than four hundred students. Indeed, the
Class of 1895 entered less than one hundred
strong. There were, however, upon the Faculty
strong and inspiring teachers who, by their
scholarship and personality, had a profound
effect upon their pupils. It will not be invidi-
ous to name two of the teachers who had an
especially marked influence upon the man who
was to be their most distinguished pupil, Anson
D. Morse and Charles E. Garman. Morse was
a very learned, wise, and essentially judicial
man, and his open-minded, judge-like treatment
of the facts of history made a strong appeal to
a man of Coolidge's mental make-up. Morse's
teaching may have confirmed in him a tendency
that has characterized him all through life,
teaching him that if one can only use deliberation, intellectual self-control, and a wise man's
balance, many serious difficulties of thought
and action vanish into thin air.

*"But it was Garman who had the most
profound effect upon Coolidge.*

Report has it that a volume containing teachings of this, Amherst's most distinguished Professor of Philosophy, has always been at hand
on Coolidge's table. Certain it is that Garman's teachings entered into the very tissue of
the thought and life of the man who is now
guiding the destinies of the country.

"Coolidge always had in him some-
thing of the philosopher.

He showed at the very outset of his college
course that he was of the reflective type, an
independent thinker; and Garman's chief object
was to develop this tendency in his pupils, to
make them handle great philosophical questions as real problems. Again and again in
Coolidge's addresses one finds evidence of
Garman in thought and expression. Consciously
or unconsciously, this teacher seems to be with
him at all times. One need only instance certain salient points in Garman's teaching to make
this clear to those who are familiar with 'Have
Faith in Massachusetts' and other public utter-
ances of the President. 'Weigh the evidence.'
'Process not product.' 'Carry all questions

back to fundamental principles.' 'The question how answers the question what.'

"Finally, if Coolidge's classmates could be consulted, they would surely agree on one thing about the man.

> *"The basis of his philosophy of life and of the way in which he has met difficult situations in his public career was ethical.*

They would agree that faith was the keynote of all that he has done. He had faith in his college, in Massachusetts, in the Nation, in great fundamental principles. He had faith that the questions which divide men must be settled on the basis of righteousness. In college, as since graduation, he was true, straightforward, frank, absolutely sure of only one thing, that truth is mighty and will prevail."

Of such then was Calvin Coolidge. He was about to plunge off the diving board of youth into the strong currents of life which were to carry him far.

CHAPTER IV

Bar, Ballots and Babes

"A wise old owl lived in an oak;
The more he saw, the less he spoke.
The less he spoke, the more he heard:
Why can't we be like that old bird?"

THIS is a story of bottles so far only as it suggests old wine of a good vintage and of a great value and of drinks of milk only, with a high respect for the eighteenth amendment, law, order and its great apostle.

Calvin Coolidge upon graduation from Amherst College returned to Plymouth, where pursuant to his always fancy he took his place upon the farm for the summer months for work and recuperation. He had come to know Northampton towards which Amherst naturally turns and fond of nature he had become attached to the natural beauty of the Connecticut Valley so that when he decided to begin the study of law it was in Northampton. Its scholastic atmosphere unconsciously drew him. When asked at

35

college where he was going to locate, he replied:

"Northampton, it's nearest."

He never went to a law school because he could
not afford to do so and he had character
enough to prosecute his studies in the atmosphere of a law office. In such an atmosphere,
the weak waver.

On September 23, 1895, he entered the office
of Hammond and Field, the leading lawyers of
the city. Curiously, the Hon. John C. Hammond, a leader of the bar, had happened to be
passing through the grove at Amherst when
Coolidge was speaking. He stopped, sat down,
stayed, listened. He welcomed him into the
office. Coolidge's investments even then paid
him the sure rate of bonds. Strangely, Edward
A. Shaw registered in the office five days later.
Coolidge as Governor put him on the Superior
Bench. This meritorious appointment has a
sentimental charm. Calvin Coolidge was admitted to the bar, July 2, 1897, after a study of
twenty months, symbolic of his application.
Then he laid down a book of compelling plot,
Blackstone's Commentaries, seldom reopened.
Those were the days before the present high

"THE EXECUTIVE MANSION." NORTHAMPTON

fixed state standards. Each applicant for the
bar could come to Suffolk, where the examina-
tions were stiffest, or appear before his own
county examiners for an oral examination.
These varied with the counties and their examiners. Some young men were qualified for practice and to jeopardize great property interests
after perhaps only diagnoses of their respira-
tion and pulse. In those days Coolidge presented himself in Hampshire County. Its standards stood high.

He never established himself as a leading
lawyer although

he was equipped with a fine legal
mind.

The opportunity was also his, under the patron-
age of such leaders as John C. Hammond and
Henry P. Field, but he followed his bent as all
young men should. A family once spent fifty
years to establish a son as a real estate operator
and failed when had he early been given his
head he would have led as a landscape gardener,
which trade they did not happen to fancy.
When Coolidge entered the office of Hammond
and Field, the former was elected District-Attor-

ney and the latter Mayor. The political atmosphere apparently was contagious. Fate pointed the path and the country lost a Chief-Justice but found a President.

As a lawyer, Coolidge had a mind which formed conclusions concisely and with originality, not merely absorbing the current wave of opinion. He did not necessarily do what "they," a mighty word, said. When he bought a hat he bought what he liked and not necessarily what he was told "they" wore. Nine men out of ten do otherwise. He was fitted for the accurate work of a learned lawyer. His life, however, so early went into the science of politics that he was not known much for his work as a lawyer.

> *The philosophy of measures and men*
> *held him most.*

His thinking on all public questions brought original, concise and accurate conclusions, which found expression in apt and unique written words. Northampton, without regard to party, has always supported him and believed in him. He early chose the science of politics in its best sense, which means statesmanship, as his study and career and from time to time avenues have opened to him so that he has been able to continue in that direction. There has been no surprise at his each advance except perhaps the last. There is a local confidence that Coolidge can carry on in the high place to which he has been called. He was always modest. When, in the office of Hammond and Field, one of his associates found, apparently mislaid in his desk, a medal which he had won in college, he asked him why he had not sent it home. He replied: "I did not think it would interest my folks." He later established the firm of Coolidge and Hemenway.

Fancy and opportunity led Coolidge into politics. He took the first logical step for any novitiate. In 1899 he served as a Councilman in Northampton, the humblest office under our form of government. This was an unpaid office and he sought this kind of a political beginning for what he could give and not for what he could get, not for recognition but for service. He established himself in the confidence of his fellow-citizens and they then proceeded to give him all they had. He began to proceed surely but steadily. He was City Solicitor in 1900 and in 1901. To one belligerent Councilman, apparently without the gift of prophecy, who boasted that he had not voted for him, Coolidge replied:

"Somebody did."

His political horizon broadened, for in 1903 he was appointed for a few months Clerk of Courts for Hampshire County. He declined an election. He was Chairman of the Republican City Committee in 1904. He was Mayor in 1910 and 1911, during a hiatus between his service as Representative and Senator. He materially cut down the municipal indebtedness. In his reading, *The Springfield Republican* became to him a Bible and, although a paper of editorial independence, he one of its saints. The long time guiding head of this paper, Solomon Bulkeley Griffin, has now retired, a patriarch of journalism of the best sort. He gave the paper a momentum which has carried it far. His ever busy mind has contributed to literature, from long years of experience with public men and measures, an interesting and invaluable record of comment and conclusion.

Calvin Coolidge met the woman who was later

to become his wife, Miss Grace Anna Goodhue, when she was a teacher in The Clark School for the Deaf at Northampton. Of this school he later became a Patron, and some wag has suggested that under him the school might with much propriety establish a branch for the dumb. When asked if she had ever been troubled by his reluctance to speak, she replied, wittily, that she had learned patience with those suffering from physical disabilities. She was the daughter of the late Andrew I. Goodhue of Burlington, Vermont, who died April 25, 1923, leaving a widow, Elmira Goodhue, the mother of Grace Anna Coolidge. He was a prominent man in the town. He was a deacon in the College Street Congregational Church and an inspector of steamboats on Lake Champlain since 1886. He had the cheer of his daughter.

Grace Goodhue was a graduate of the Burlington High School in 1897, where she read a paper on

"The Tramp Instinct,"

which apparently reconciled her mind to the trail for the White House. She graduated from the University of Vermont in 1902. She is an admirable complement to the President. When if he seeks to fuse with the people, she is his vital link. She is a successful blender. She is of attractive appearance. She has a bright mind. She tactfully declines to commit herself on public questions that she may not embarrass her husband.

The courtship of Coolidge was unique. Should he have sought letters patent on it, it would not have been litigated. They must have been drawn towards one another by their apparently utter diversity. He laid much confidence on the power of propinquity, sitting and silence. In the stress of rivalry he bought a pair of skates, but he wore them once only, as he was unable to maintain the pace. When he sought to bring the campaign to a climax, he presented himself before Andrew Goodhue. He said: "I've come to marry Grace." "Does she know it," he was asked. "No," he replied, "Not now, but she will." On this great question, Andrew Goodhue and his wife Elmira, after taking an inventory of the future President, preserved an attitude of strict neutrality which would have thrilled even Woodrow Wilson. Asked once by a representative of the

press for the romance of her marriage, Grace
Goodhue Coolidge replied: "Have you ever
seen my husband?"

There could have been, however, but one out-
come to the campaign. Calvin Coolidge had
never been repulsed. When the hour ripened
for action, he gently spread a kerchief upon
the carpeted floor on Maple Street. With characteristic foresight even then he sought to protect his right pant, for trousers were not in those
days worn in Burlington, as he knelt before his
ideal. He put to her a question, great for him,
simple for her. He is a man of honor. He laid
before her his disabilities.

*He confided to her alone that Fate
had pointed to the Presidency for him.*

With rare tact, respecting his vagaries, she
replied in a monosyllable: "Yes." They were
married, October 4, 1905. If Grace Anna
Goodhue Coolidge has ever deplored her de-
cision, she has had too much loyalty to the
President to betray it. She is a woman of
charm, tact and efficiency. Although unrecognized by public office, she has as large an
interest as any one in the Calvin Grace Coolidge

Company, of which the President is, of course, a silent partner. When Calvin Coolidge came into the Presidency of the United States, he came into his second greatest honor and responsibility. He had for eighteen years been already acclimated.

The Coolidges have two sons, John Coolidge, born September 7, 1906, and Calvin Coolidge, Junior, born April 13, 1908. The boys have been educated in a democratic atmosphere at the public schools in Northampton and are now at Mercersburg Academy in Pennsylvania preparing, of course, for Amherst College. John is like his mother, Calvin like his father. John was at the Devens Camp in August, 1923, although he was under age. The father is an admirable judge of capacity. John has a high respect for his father and knows this. In acknowledging a simple gift, John wrote the donor:

"Father says you are a great man and
ought to be in Washington."

It would be improper to identify the donor more than to say that he is his first biographer. Calvin Coolidge, Junior, worked upon a tobacco field at Hatfield in the summer of 1923 for three dollars and one-half a day. He apparently made a good trade for a boy. When asked about his father, he said: "Yes, I suppose he is President. Which shed shall I work in?" He has not inherited garrulity. Both boys have, however, inherited the spirit of preparation.

The family are members of the Edwards Congregational Church in Northampton. Before the Men's Club of this church, Coolidge once asked one of his legislative colleagues to speak. He is a wit and he lamented in his opening that a college town should have sent to the Senate, an office which is respected at least in Boston, such a noisy and otherwise undesirable man as Coolidge. One of his audience, after the talk, who knew Coolidge, of course, with a fine sense of humor, said to the speaker: "Young man, seeing that Coolidge got you this opportunity, I think you have spoken of him in very poor taste."

The Coolidges have always lived simply. The President continues to vote in Northampton, where the family have one-half of a double wooden house at twenty-one Massasoit Street.

His salary as President is seventy-five thousand
dollars a year. His Northampton house rental
is thirty-two dollars a month, recently raised
from thirty. He lives within his income, it is
thought, apparently with reason.

The family might with some reason
adopt as its crest a Cal-la lily.

His landlord is ready to evict his other tenant
for any one who can prove that he has been, is
or will be President of the United States.

Over the fireplace at Northampton are the
words which introduce this dissertation on
Bar, Ballots and Babes,

undoubtedly the inspiration of
our hero.

CHAPTER V

HIS UNOFFICIAL LIFE

CALVIN COOLIDGE became of age, July 4, 1893. He held no public office until 1899. He was also in private life in 1902, 1905, 1906 and 1909. These years, after July 2, 1897, when he was admitted to the bar, he practiced law exclusively. He is now in his fourteenth consecutive year as an office-holder. In thirty years, he has held public office, twenty-one years.

Again, not a story of quantity.

CHAPTER VI

Up Beacon Hill

*"And while the tired waves vainly
    breaking
Seem here no painful inch to gain,
Far back through creek and inlet making
Comes silent flooding in the main."*
                                    —*Clough.*

THIS is a story of progress and of patience,
the story of the pendulum, one tick at a time,
the story of the ladder, one round at a time,
no jumps. It is a short story and a thrilling
story. It ought to stimulate the conviction in
the heart of every young American that
America is a democracy of the right sort, the
country of law, order and opportunity and that
the greatest office known to civilization is within
his grasp if only he shapes his course for the
stars.

Calvin Coolidge is essentially a politician,
a dangerous term which is much abused.
Augustus Peabody Gardner, Congressman and
soldier, A Pioneer for Preparedness, was a
politician and he boasted that he was. Where

48

COOLIDGE AND HIS FIRST BIOGRAPHER TAKEN TOGETHER

Five Years Legislative Colleagues

Committee on Railroads — 1913

Senate Chairman   House Chairman

he led, any one should hope to follow. A politician is one who seeks to live out the study of government and of men. It is as high-minded an aspiration to seek to save a country in times of peace by the ballot as in times of war by the bullet. The best estimate of Calvin Coolidge is not as a farmer or as a lawyer but as a politician, for this is his trade.

In January, 1907, Coolidge turned from the half-mile track of city politics to the Grand Circuit on Beacon Hill. He was in appearance and inclinations much as he is today. He was sparse of structure; and sparse of hair, which with growing modesty had dulled into a quieter shade. He was a well-read man. There was nothing about him to startle or to draw any one who simply looked at him. He was still a Vermonter with a Yankee twang. This apparently troubled him little, for he has never attempted to revise it. His voice qualifies more for an executive chamber than for the hustings. It will never jeopardize in opera the memory of the late Enrico Caruso. Some close to him say that he is proud of it. The Lord loveth whom He chasteneth and the Scriptures abound not only in the virtues but also in the faults of the prophets. He is a *tout ensemble,* which, while it might be looked upon with some suspicion at Lenox or at Newport, has proved itself an asset at the ballot box.

Coolidge had come to sit in the Massachusetts House for two years, 1907 and 1908, to be stirred and stimulated by its traditions. Here hangs the sacred codfish, symbolic curiously of a State then great in its fisheries but now great in its manufactures. There might well also hang there in these days a spindle and a bobbin.

Lord Bryce says that there is no greater legislative body, in its dignity and efficiency.

Strangely, the electorate are quick to spatter it, forgetting that they only spatter themselves, for they create it. It is as great and as small as the people, for it represents the people, who elect it. In it are the straight and the sinuous, the bee and the sluggard, the pulchritudinous and the plain, the scintillating and the stupid, the well and the sick. The same men are found inside as are found outside, and now more than one woman, like pansies among weeds.

The Herald.   C. C.   R. M. W.

THE MASSACHUSETTS LEGISLATURE
The Mock Session, June 20, 1913

A Human Lapse

An office, great or small, is what the man who holds it makes it. The most forgotten blade of grass in the most distant district has some one to protect it. The incoming legislator is awed by the atmosphere. When he is first recognized by the Speaker, he stutters, stammers and stumbles. He is overpowered by the Speaker on his splendid dais. He forgets that he is only human, and that towards eventide he sits perhaps in unprotected hose like some other men. No one who has sat there would have sat elsewhere. It is a hall of legislation, primarily. It is a house of human nature, anecdotes, friendships which abound and long linger. It is a great clubhouse maintained by the State at one-half million dollars a year, where an audience always awaits and more, a gallery. Those were "halycon" days said one alumnus, careless of his diction in his affectionate retrospection.

Coolidge on reaching Boston went from The North Station on foot to The Adams House, the Mecca of all west State politicians. When he had superscribed the register and for the first time had heard the word,

"front,"

no one watched him, crossed over to read his
name, pursuant to the practice of hostelries and
to look at him. He was assigned to an upper
inner chamber looking out, not onto Mount
Washington or the Atlantic but into an inner
area. He was not assigned to the Presidential
suite nor would he have been had he owned
the hotel. He was happier where he was in
an atmosphere of simplicity. Few sought him,
which welcome he was content to reciprocate
with even drooping warmth, this with no effort.
Had he found the print of a foot upon the mat
before his door, he would have experienced
emotions akin to those of the derelict Crusoe
when he found upon the sands the marks of the
savage.

He was then as he is today and he was not
elected President of the United States then
because he was not known. He had to be known
to be appreciated. He was taciturn then as
today but he spoke with a wise caution and
often what he said was touched up with a
Lincolnesque humor which gave much satisfaction to those who sat about him, that is
when he was not alone as he often was. He
was less slow to respond to a question than

to initiate communion. When he lunched, it was not at The Bellevue with Tom White and other *bon vivants*. No one seemed to know where he ate. When he ate, however, if he ate, he was true to Vermont and its traditions, for when the luncheon drew near to the tooth-picks he was sure to order placed before him a piece of pie and, not a demi-tasse but a large cup of coffee. These are infallible tests of the Vermont thoroughbred.

> *He moved then as now, always quietly like a high-grade motor fresh from the factory. There were no loose bolts. There was no scarcity of lubricant.*

He was apparently indifferent as to whether his name was displayed on the front pages of the press or close to the mortuary column, and perhaps happier when placed in the latter space. When at rare intervals he was asked to join a motor party, he sat in silence in the "bin" over intervals of miles, recognizing no obligation to light up his playmates, his intellect fixed, apparently content in listening, thinking and maintaining the draft in what by courtesy

may be called a cigar, not a perfecto. He
simply flopped. In his own words, "I have not
been hurt by what I have not said." He was
seldom found supine upon the benches of the
rotunda which abounded in his colleagues, but
he could have been often located by any cour-
ageous explorer in his own boudoir, reading
a book or a paper, gazing in thought out of
the window, perhaps at a ventilator, or even
lying on the bed for recuperation. For he
never forgot the day that was to come, body
and mind. Had The League of Nations become
the power it was planned, he would not have
dallied with the Presidency but he would have
stepped immediately to the head of that great
association. He was never emotional, always
stoical, never angry, always courteous. Such
he was. Such he is. As he grew in strength,
his constituency grew in versatility.

> *All men seemed to be with him and*
> *there marched behind him an army.*
> *High potentates of the church com-*
> *manded one wing and "The Black*
> *Horse Cavalry" the other.*

In the same dilution in which Roosevelt said

he digested Platt, so our hero was never skit-
tish about his playmates whether they taught
Sunday school or not so long as they could
help in a cause which looked good to him. He
was a mystery then, even to those who thought
they knew him.

He is a mystery now.

This augments his political availability and he
probably knows, recognizes and values it.

When the Legislature convened, Calvin Coolidge was presented to Martin Lomasney, looked
upon as a fashionable procedure. It is popular to daub Lomasney in the back "deestricts"
as a dangerous citizen. His hair is wasted
enough, however, to show that he wears no horns
and his feet are shaped quite regularly. Martin looked upon the boy, attempting to classify
him as he does every one, wondering as he says
whether he was a school teacher or an under-
taker. If he diagnosed him wisely at that early
day, it was as a Ford car with a Pierce motor.

Coolidge did not come to Boston unarmed
but with a letter of introduction to the then
Speaker, John N. Cole. He was a great pre-
siding officer, so was the Hon. John L. Bates,

none greater. This introduction was in the matter of his committee appointments, borne by young legislators fresh from the egg, pursuant to the practice of the times. It is to be hoped that this letter was sealed when it was handed to him by his fellow townsman, the Hon. Richard W. Irwin, now a Judge of the Superior Court, for it read in this way, simply:

> *"He's better than he looks, like a*
> *singed cat."*

In 1911 Irwin had no more sincere endorser for his elevation to the bench than Calvin Coolidge. He became the first of his fellow citizens to sleep in "the spare-room" at the White House. This letter was read in the spirit in which it was written, for John Cole later appointed Coolidge to the Committee on Judiciary. This was the place he wanted, if he wanted any place. With this place he was content as he was always content, for he never forced a controversy, although he was ever ready to take a stand on the issues which came his way. Hence he had bided his time for coming to the House from Northampton, when he could come without opposition. And a Republican, he came from a district which was then Democratic.

It is significant of the man that a member of his capacity should have never received a House Chairmanship, or have been put on Judiciary until his second year. This was because his nature could not impress, immediately, its virtues on those around him, and he saw this and he was content to wait for the time when they would become known and recognized.

In his service in the House he was respected. He showed his independence.

He took a firm stand for a small, independent oil refiner named Hisgen of Springfield in a bill which was strenuously opposed by the great Standard Oil Company. He was instrumental in getting on the books an anti-monopoly law and his work in codifying the banking laws of the State was also of far-reaching importance. If any of his colleagues in those days had dared to foretell that he would have been elected Governor, he would have been retired to a retreat. In his service he was content to do the day's work. He did not seek the notice of the press or of any one. He was not looked upon as a

leader of the House, where such men as Cushing, Norman White, Walker and now Congressman Luce were prominent. He was a child of
Vermont. He was proud of her although he had
a high respect for his step-mother, Massachusetts. When a Senator interested in legislation
ventured into the House, Coolidge lavished his
twang upon his seat-mate:

> *"What's he maousin' 'raound the*
> *Haouse for?"*

In his journeys between Northampton and the
Capitol, he always travelled the so-called back
way, not by Springfield but through Ware, Barre
and Holden. He looked out of the car windows,
not for factories but for farms. He became a
familiar figure on the trains. At the end of
1908 he retired to Northampton.

> *He had not yet churned his wake*
> *white.*

In 1912 Calvin Coolidge came to Beacon
Hill again and to stay. He served then in the
Senate for four years, the last two as President.
Pursuant to his policy of patience, he had de-
layed his candidacy and his return until his

predecessor, the Hon. Allen T. Treadway, boniface and Congressman, had served his customary three years as President of the Senate and voluntarily retired. Calvin Coolidge was unwilling to crowd him or anybody. When some one lamented to him the size of his district and the difficulty of covering it, he replied: "It's just as hard for my opponent." While a member of the upper branch, he never made trouble for his Senate President, his Governor or any one. He looked upon himself as a cog in the government, to do his part, to follow the leaders.

He never sought to make history for himself. Most men seek to do little else, their country second, if at all.

In 1912, his first year as Senator, he performed a signal service as Chairman of the Special Legislative Committee on Reconciliation. This committee was formed to take jurisdiction of the Lawrence strike. Coolidge met the situation with tact, efficiency and solution. Industrial peace was reëstablished. In 1913 the second year of his service, he was made Chairman of the Committee on Railroads, no more important appointment. Again significantly this rec-

ognition did not come to him immediately.
Nothing did. As a member of the Senate he
secured the passage of the anti-discrimination
law which has proved of great advantage. He
backed "the full crew bill" and since that time
has had the united support of the train men. In
those days the Railroad Committee had jurisdiction over the great question of the legislative
year, the New Haven issue. He listened much.
He said little. His humor stood by him, like
Abraham Lincoln. At one of the hearings, a
feverish petitioner had suggested that Charles
Sanger Mellen be sent to jail, a popular pastime
in those days. It must bring the former Colos-
sus of Roads much innocent amusement to note,
that his great policies, which the government
opposed then, it favors now. At that hearing
a participant, who wore his hair pompadour in
his zeal as a child of the people, said: "Mr.
Mellen, if I were Governor you would not thrive
in Massachusetts five minutes." Then Mellen
replied, in his soft voice, and he was a master
with the rapier: "Perhaps, Mr. ——, that's the
reason you are not Governor." The art of irony
has a strong back-kick which did much to locate
permanently Mr. Mellen in Council Grove. He

was ready to pay the price. All such artists are.
To go back, this feverish petitioner then said to
the Chairman that he would retire unless he
desired to interrogate him further. Then Coolidge said: "Retire, unless you are willing to
remain and protect the Committee from these
railroad lawyers present." One of his coarse
colleagues once approached him, irreverently:
"Cal," said he in the crude colloquial, "loosen
up, lapse, humanize yourself and lunch with
me, today." Coolidge simply nodded, No.
About noon he motioned to him to approach, with
this enthusiastic invitation, sotto voce: "Mrs.
Coolidge and I lunch at The Bellevue at one,

Come, if you want."

It was impossible to resist. Invited to speak
at the opening of the Town Hall in Weston he
was asked what he was going to say. He replied: "I do not know," and then later produced
a manuscript which he read.

He was always a student, always prepared,
always looking forward. He showed an unlim-
ited familiarity with the bills before his Com-
mittees, going in 1913 before The Ways and
Means Committee with an elaborate bill which

his Committee on Railroads had reported, the so-called Washburn Bill, and talking on it from all angles as intelligently as the counsel who had been hired to study it. To his then House-Chairman of the Committee, with reference to an attitude he had taken on a bill before them, he wrote:

"Sand your tracks, you're slipping."

He was Chairman of the Committee on Resolutions at Worcester, at a Republican convention, October 3, 1914, which nominated the Hon. Samuel W. McCall for Governor. At one of its hearings when he was asked a pointed question, he twirled his chair towards the window and looked out in silence. Some one said to Governor McCall, who stood near by: "I could take dictation from that man and in long hand." The Governor often tells this story. Coolidge did not remain to mix with the delegates at the hotel and his host found him later in his bed, the door ajar, with his trousers or rather pants suspended thereupon, to maintain their contour.

In 1914 and 1915 he was President of the Senate. In 1913 the then President, the Hon.

Levi Greenwood, a splendid political colt, was unexpectedly defeated for reëlection. Within two days of his defeat, Coolidge was assured of the succession. What he wanted he got, because it came. When he was President of the State Senate, he sought to soothe one Walter E. McLane, also a Senator, it is thought by some since his return from the War of 1812. He must have been born on Beacon Hill. Walter had been told by a colleague to go where clothes are bought last and ice first. Cal said: "Walter, I have found time to examine the Constitution and the Senate Rules. There's nothing in them to compel you to go."

No lines are more significant in explaining Calvin Coolidge than these which follow:

"Although I am Coolidge's friend, and have been for years," he said, *"I did not really understand him, until about a year ago. One day he came in here, and, after sitting where you are for the longest time, he said, out of a clear sky: 'Do you know, I've never really grown up? It's a hard thing for me to play this game. In politics, one must meet people, and that's not easy for me.' I expressed astonish-*

ment. 'No,' he went on, 'it's been hard for me all my life. When I was a little fellow, as long ago as I can remember, I would go into a panic if I heard stranger voices in the house. I felt I just couldn't meet the people and shake hands with them. Most of the visitors would sit with Mother and Father in the kitchen and the hardest thing in the world was to have to go through the kitchen door and give them a greeting. I was almost ten before I realized I couldn't go on that way. And by fighting hard I used to manage to get through that door. I'm all right with old friends, but every time I meet a stranger, I've got to go through the old kitchendoor, back home, and it's not easy.' He was silent for a long time after that. Just sat looking out of the window. Then he went away without another word. He's never mentioned the subject since. Nor have I, but I think I can say I understand Calvin Coolidge now. Does it help to explain him to you?"

When he appears cold, he is diffident. No man understands Calvin Coolidge unless he recognizes his silence. No one understands his silence unless he recognizes as its original cause

his original diffidence.   This silence he has been
slow to eliminate because his serious attitude
towards life has made him slow to interrupt a
life of much thought for a life of any chatter.

On the inside, he is warm.

At a luncheon of Republican leaders at a country club, when the party was about to start for
Norumbega Park, the whole procession was held
up until Edward Horrigan, his bodyguard,
could locate in an obscure part of the house
an humble friend of the Governor to ride
with him.   One day as the Governor was
starting from The Adams House for the Governor's Walk across the Common to the State
House with Horrigan, the former was pointed
out to a stranger in the town.   "He's a fine looking man," he commented, "but who's the little
red-headed feller with him?"   It was Ed Horrigan's duty to protect the Governor from hunters.
Hence naturally a wit suggested that he ought
to be interested in a bill which was filed in the
Legislature for a permanent close season on red
foxes.

In 1916, 1917 and 1918, Calvin Coolidge was
Lieutenant-Governor.   At three o'clock on the

afternoon following his first election, when most
successful candidates were easily congratulated
in public places, he was found alone in that inside room at The Adams House, sitting by an
open window. In these days, the typical candidate who has reconciled his mind to holding
high public office continues to pursue the voter.
He effusively simulates a desire to share his
cross. He seeks to locate the strawberry-mark
which identifies the long lost brother. As against
him, the personality of Calvin Coolidge pre-
sents a marked, restful and delicious contrast.
He has never forgotten that if one would have
the respect of others he must respect himself.
He has taught the voter to recognize the value of
pursuing what is not pursuing him. Calvin
Coolidge was then, as later, loyal to his Chief,
the Governor, and sympathetic, and unlike some
of his predecessors he showed no impatience for
preferment.   The Hon. Samuel Walker McCall
has the record of a scholarly statesman.   He
has a fine literary capacity.   His pen is a wand.
He is essentially a Doctor of Letters.   He was
War Governor of the State.   He was for years a
Congressman from a university district.   He has
had a creditable record.   He says that Coolidge

as Lieutenant-Governor was loyal to him in letter and in spirit. He adds: "He was with me in the Council even when the votes stood seven to two."

*Coolidge was content to do, in his own
words, the day's work.*

While most men in the public service starve for public notice and recognition, he was content to keep the traces taut, and knee-action and the spectacular appeal of the leader in the tandem had no charm for him. He had established his qualities, humor, sound sense, taciturnity, modesty and character. He had become a statesman. According to that eminent divine, the Reverend George Angier Gordon, D. D.:

*"No man can be a statesman without
character."*

Strangely, a unique specimen like Coolidge has as many as two doubles and in one State, in form if not in substance. The delusion they betray by their comparative freedom of speech. One is the Hon. Richard Bradford Coolidge, Mayor of Medford. Since August 3, 1923, he has been a student of genealogy, hoping to discover a common branch with the President. The other is Robert Washburn Maynard, a son of the late Rear-Admiral. Frank Stearns, unconsciously attracted toward him, took him into the bottom of his business. He has pushed him like a son. He saw the replica. He has put him at the top of his business. Since Maynard began to write his name in full he has come fast.

Coolidge was nominated for Governor in the fall of 1918, Samuel W. McCall having served the customary three years. When he was ready to retire, Coolidge was ready to proceed.

He had not sought to facilitate his preferment by a critical attitude of his superiors.

He believed in Republicanism and in harmony and was content to go up or down with his party. He was elected Governor and served as such in 1919 and 1920. He made an admirable record. His first act was to appoint as his Secretary the Hon. Henry F. Long, of capacity and tact. It was almost a pleasure to burden him. When the Governor retired, he did not forget to place Henry Long in a comfortable official nest, after the manner of all Governors. He showed sound sense in his appointments. In his first year as

Governor the business system of the Commonwealth was reorganized and the Governor cut
one hundred and seventeen commissions down
to twenty, pursuant to the action of the Constitutional Convention of 1918. This delicate
duty, involving many appointments and some
removals, was done as well as any human could
do it, though some good men fell by the way.

*With characteristic loyalty, he
wrote his step-mother at Plymouth, regularly,*

preoccupied as he was with his pressing public
duties and often sent her flowers. When the
police strike broke, he immediately wrote her
what course he should take, which he did take.
As Governor he was conservative and yet his
mind was always open to forward suggestions.
These were not "progressive," for progressive is
a tired term and should be retired to rest and
all Republicans should be known either as
Backward or Forward Republicans.

As to his personal characteristics as Governor,
for the public is always interested in the daily
lives of its servants, he brushed his hair regularly and his teeth. He ate when hungry. He

slept when tired. These concessions to an
electorate, hard to satiate in its scrutiny of the
great, who in many ways are much like them.
Of his toilets today when his wardrobe is
at the peak, he has three gowns, a blue and a
gray, business gowns, and a black morning coat
much worn by Coolidge inaugurals. These are
outside the smock-frock at Plymouth, which is
also worn outside, and in which he reviews the
live stock on the farm. He is vulnerable in the
raiment about the base of his head where it
meets the body, or in easy English, his neck.
Here it must be confessed the points of his collar
shun each other and the tie droops. Fifty cents
and a pin, a collar of the Welch-Margetson type
which meets and the pin deftly used to hold the
tie, high, would make him an ideal feature on
the landscape of society. Surely he ought to
respond, in the exigencies of The White House.

Representatives of the press who thought that
they interviewed him, interviewed themselves.
He has always apparently been indifferent as to
whether he was personally liked or not. It
would be a solace to a much pursued public if
more public men would emulate this characteristic. His wit he has always sought to stifle, for

he has seen this quality destroy many men who would have been great. It has been a strange sensation to a Legislature which has seen surrounding it men with the personal charm of Warren, Storrs and the late Ralph D. Gillette, coming out of the West, to find in Coolidge one whose qualifications were of merit only. He never attacks men and seldom things. His creed is that progress is best made by emphasizing good policies and ignoring evil ones.

As Governor, Coolidge continued to live as he always had, at The Adams House, with the same panorama before the same windows of the same inside upper chamber. When he last packed his bag as retiring Governor and slammed that door, he was much the same as when he first came into the room as Representative Coolidge, except that he had marked his qualities upon Beacon Hill and they were recognized.

It was sweet praise of Calvin Coolidge when his successor, His Excellency, Channing Harris Cox, then set out to aspire not only to carry out but even to perfect the policies of his predecessor, Calvin the Silent. He then consecrated as one of his Secretaries a young man surnamed Stiller. While Coolidge is warm on the inside,

Cox is warm on the outside. The last hope of the former is to warm those who park close to the official desk. It is the first realization of the latter. Neither of them is Massachusetts born. It will be exceedingly unfashionable and difficult to elect in 1924 a Massachusetts-born Governor.

In 1919, Coolidge was honored with the degrees of LL.D. by Amherst, Tufts and Williams; and in 1920 by Bates, University of Vermont and Wesleyan. When he was welcomed to Vermont on Commencement Day as a son-in-law, he emphasized the untraditional warmth of the relation. As an evidence of his versatility, he is a member of the Corinthian Yacht and the Tennis and Racquet Clubs, among other clubs.

He is the author of "Have Faith in Massachusetts." Calvin Coolidge should have faith in Massachusetts for each is under an obligation to the other. She has done much for him.

If Calvin Coolidge has not faith in Massachusetts, who should have?

CHAPTER VII

THE TWO ALLIES

*Capacity is quick to see and to
seize opportunity.*

AN analysis of the conditions which turned
Calvin Coolidge towards the Vice-Presidency is
vital in a consideration of his success and its
causes.

Boswell did much to make Johnson. Mark
Hanna, with the physical vigor and mental determination which made him a leader in the
iron industry, did much to make McKinley.
To him he was a vital complement. The only
man who always honestly and cheerfully wor-
ships his creator is the self-made man. A
public servant who has been appointed to public
office on the petition of strong endorsers is often
quick to evade the obligation and to nurse the
delusion that his is simply a recognition of
virtues which could not be evaded. Luck has
been defined as the capacity to seize opportunity. Opportunity knocks at some doors
often, at others once only, at others not at all.

There are many able, even brilliant men who
have never sat in a motor of their own because
they have been unable to see and to seize that
market where their product may be best sold.

> *The President has always been quick*
> *to seize opportunity with capacity.*
> *He is the finished product of a tri-*
> *umvirate: Calvin Coolidge, Frank*
> *Waterman Stearns and Edwin Upton*
> *Curtis, led by Fate.*

Calvin Coolidge would have been President of
the United States had these two men never lived.
It had been decreed. They simply hurried his
feet. They were the hand-maidens of Fate.

One whole paragraph is here deservedly and
cheerfully conceded to Frank Waterman Stearns.
He is a leading merchant of Boston and the
son of one. His capacity and loyalty are exceeded only by his modesty. He forgets only
himself. He has the respect and friendship of
men who have established themselves in business, professional life and politics, and his
mother has contributed a son to the ministry.
His business Mecca is an autographed gallery
where the first portrait placed and seen is of

HIS FIRST ALLY
FRANK WATERMAN STEARNS

Calvin Coolidge. Having made himself, his delight is to make others. Calvin Coolidge and he are both graduates of Amherst College, their first bond, and both are now trustees. Frank Stearns first fastened his eye on Calvin Coolidge when a petitioner for legislation for Amherst College he sought him on Beacon Hill through another. Then the mercury of Coolidge was poured upon his representative in its most shrivelled form, a fine type as an emaciated exhibit. Frank Stearns wondered. He was troubled. He retired. His curiosity was stimulated. He studied him. He came to believe in him and to admire and to worship him. When he ponders him the first commandment is in jeopardy. His faith in Calvinism was first diagnosed by some as an obsession and then accepted by them as a religion. He is the only living American, if any one outside of the Coolidge kin, to understand the President, for he puzzles and appeals by the charm of mystery, not the least of his assets.

Frank Waterman Stearns is the first of The Two Allies who have done much to reveal Calvin Coolidge into the Vice-Presidency.

Frank Waterman Stearns in an interview with Theodore G. Joslin, the accomplished Washington correspondent of *The Boston Transcript*, says, in part:

"I first met the President in 1915, when he was President of the Massachusetts Senate. Some time later I sent a classmate of mine at Amherst College to Mr. Coolidge to ask for his help in getting through a bill to make it possible to connect the college power system with the Amherst town system. Mr. Coolidge would promise nothing, and we felt quite disappointed that an Amherst man and a Senator from a district next to that in which Amherst is should show so little interest. When we went to have the bill taken up the following year, we found it had been passed and was law. Mr. Coolidge did it. We learned afterwards that when we first asked his aid it was too late in the session to obtain action that year. What impressed me was his refusal to promise, but his readiness to act when the time came.

"This made me curious, and I made many inquiries about him and learned all I could about his record.

What I learned convinced me that he
was even then one of the ablest men
of our generation.

The thought came to me not then but when he
was Lieutenant-Governor, that here was a man
with all the qualities necessary to make a great
President, and I cannot tell exactly why or
how the conviction came to me that he would
some day be President.

"He once told me that when he was elected
to the Legislature in Massachusetts he was regarded as one who would work for reforms of
various kinds. He became quickly convinced
that

administration was far behind
legislation,

as he put it, and that it was his duty to be
conservative. I think he thought this may have
disappointed some, but he was resolved that
it was the right course, and held to it. I have
the feeling that it was the right course and
still hold to it.

"I persuaded him to be the guest of honor
at a dinner I gave about that time at The Algon-
quin Club in Boston. There were about forty

or fifty men of standing in the community
present. This dinner was to enable those attend-
ing to express their appreciation of what Mr.
Coolidge had done up to that time, and he
was quite surprised to learn he had attracted
so much interest.

"After that dinner I began urging him to be
a candidate for the Republican nomination for
Lieutenant-Governor. It was a most difficult
task. The Legislature was in session and I got
no response. After the Legislature had ad-
journed I was with him one night at dinner.
He handed me a piece of paper on which was
written,

> *'I am a candidate for Lieutenant-
> Governor, Calvin Coolidge.'*

He told me I could give it to the newspapers.
I asked him why he had delayed so long. I
recalled to him that a gentleman of high standing in the community had been a candidate
for almost a year and I felt that the delay had
injured us. 'Can't you see that any other course
would not have been the right one,' he said.
'The Legislature was in session, and if I had
announced my candidacy, then, every word and

action of mine would have been twisted. Legislation would have been in a mess. The public business would have suffered. I had to take that chance.'

"When Mr. Coolidge was Lieutenant-Governor I met him often at luncheon in the Parker House in Boston. I arranged to have two or three men there to meet him, so that they could know him and appreciate him, as I did, and so that he might have the benefit of their ideas.

*Some of them were puzzled at
Mr. Coolidge's silence,*

and I doubted if they made any impression upon him. I mention this to bring out one of Mr. Coolidge's principal characteristics. This is his patience of investigation, his slowness of getting the facts, but his quickness of action. A man might tell him something, be disappointed or puzzled at his reticence, go off to play golf or do something else, and learn on his return that Mr. Coolidge had acted. He had peculiar ability to judge the effect of legislation, not in the immediate future but in the time to come.

*His thought is for the long, the per-
manent good and not for the demand
of the present.*

"Another thing that always impressed me
about Mr. Coolidge is that

he is a profound student.

He studies to improve himself, to obtain knowledge with which to deal with questions coming
before him and to make his study effective in
government.

"I naturally know of Mr. Coolidge's problems in the Boston police strike, and should
like to say that he never thought his course
would win him any political advantage. It was
never in his mind.

*I know that he wrote a private letter,
during those critical days, outlining
the course he intended to follow —
and did — and saying it would very
possibly mean his elimination from
politics.*

The police strike did not make Mr. Coolidge,
as some have said, thoughtlessly. As the Rev.
Dr. Edward T. Sullivan of Newton said, in a ser-

mon at the time, the crisis did not make Mr.
Coolidge, it revealed him. He was able to
rise to and meet the emergency thrust upon him

> *because he had kept the faith in*
> *small things.*

Dr. Sullivan said: 'Those who know him best
realize that his action in this crisis was just
the working out of the character in him.'

"As I came to know Mr. Coolidge I began
to feel sure of certain things with regard to
him.

> *First, I found him splendidly honest.*

He has been placed in a good many trying
positions, where, if there was a yellow streak
in him, it would almost certainly have come
out. Perhaps the best summary of Coolidge's
character, as I read it, is, that, among the clever
orators, eager reformers and shrewd politicians
by whom he is surrounded, he seems to me to
be the one man whose thought and work are all
constructive. That is what I, in common with
many others, have been looking for: that is what
I believe I have found in Mr. Coolidge.

*"Mr. Coolidge is a real progressive in
the best sense of the word.*

A minister of my acquaintance once preached
a sermon in which he said that what appears
to be progress is quite often retrogression. He
cited an example of a man making great haste
toward the west when his real destination was
the east, and said that the faster this man went
the less progress he was making. Mr. Coolidge
once said to me that he knows the world moves,
and he wishes to move with it, but that he de-
sires to know where he is going and not retro-
gress by stepping off into a large puddle.
Another thing about Mr. Coolidge — he is able
to keep his mind on the actual question and
does not allow himself to become confused with
extraneous issues.

"I have always felt that, with very few ex-
ceptions, Mr. Coolidge is better known generally
throughout the country than any other man. It
is not that people know much about him but that
what they know suits them and gives them a
correct picture of the man.

"I think this was shown conclusively when
he became President, when there was so little

apprehension over his succession. There was,
on the other hand, widespread confidence in
him. Since he became President he has received
thousands of messages and the significant thing
about them is that so many declare they have
full confidence in him.

*"I think that one of the many causes for
the gratitude we owe Mr. Harding is that he
made Mr. Coolidge, in effect, a member of his
Cabinet, with the result, that Mr. Coolidge is
thoroughly posted on conditions as they stand,
today."*

One plain paragraph. This, gentle reader,
that you may understand some of the ways in
which Frank Waterman Stearns was an efficient
ally to Calvin Coolidge and how you may intelligently either shape your own political
course or retire to obscurity. He is a successful business man, skilled in the art of
organization. Hence his counsel is wise. He
did much to spread through the country, "Have
Faith in Massachusetts." Further, he controls
a business which means much advertising in
the columns of the press. The press has never
sought to smother in its news and editorial
columns such men as he. Hence, when Stearns

spoke Coolidge, the press printed Coolidge. Gentle reader, have you ever noted that when you have made a speech, which, in your opinion has shadowed Webster, and you have feverishly searched the press, it has reported you somewhat in these words: "Percy Alwin also spoke." Perhaps, when if you work, you are a member of the bar or a veterinary. If you would proceed more rapidly, politically, then open a garage or enter into some other business which means advertising. If you will make your commercial business profitable to the press, then it is less unlikely to make political preferment impossible for you. Is there not a political son-rise now threatening in Massachusetts, nurtured in part by advertising in the columns of the press. Ponder these sordid suggestions. Incidentally, Coolidge often looked into the business office of Stearns, where a sizeable correspondence was typed ready for his signature. These are some of the things Stearns did for Coolidge, on top of what he modestly admits. Reader, do you now understand, in a way, what Stearns has done for Coolidge? Have you any friends like him or even one like him? Can you not understand why Calvin Coolidge has faith, not only in Massachusetts, but also in Frank Waterman Stearns? Each has done much for him. This is a plain paragraph. His First Biography is an honest biography. A biography which is not an honest biography is no biography and valueless except perhaps for the next of kin of whom it writes.

Edwin Upton Curtis, now dead, was a citizen of Boston. He was a graduate of Bowdoin, a great son and trustee of the college. He commanded his time, which he gave to the public service. He was a stalwart Republican. He had been Mayor of Boston, Collector of the Port and a Metropolitan Park Commissioner. His dominant virtues were a clear head, determination and efficiency. He knew not fear.

He did much to glorify the administration of Calvin Coolidge.

At 5.45 P.M., Tuesday, September 9, 1919, Edwin Upton Curtis was Police Commissioner of the City of Boston under appointment by Samuel W. McCall, a former Governor. Two-thirds of the police of the city had then unionized. Edwin Upton Curtis had issued an order that all men in the service should not unionize.

The order reads:

"19. No member of the force shall join or belong
to any organization, club or body composed of present or present and past members of the force which
is affiliated with or a part of any organization, club
or body outside the department, except that a post of
the Grand Army of the Republic, the United Spanish
War Veterans and the American Legion of World's
War Veterans may be formed within the department."

This order was promulgated by him under an
authorization by the Legislature for the government of the police in his discretion. This order
they had refused to respect. He had then tried
and suspended nineteen of the force who were
officers of the union. Then the police, this
fraction, went on strike. The men repudiated
the order and demanded reinstatement. The
Commissioner demanded that the order should
be respected and refused to reinstate the striking police. This was the issue. The fire of
the enemy was first fastened upon him. There
was no hesitation on his part from the first.
He established his position. He stood firm, to
his everlasting honor and in jeopardy of his
life, for to him in his condition any form of
excitement was fraught with danger. He was
the Belgium, and, with the Governor, the Marne

of the situation. A statue is to be erected on
The Esplanade in Boston, for which the people
have subscribed, in honor of Edwin Upton
Curtis.

> *Edwin Upton Curtis was the second
> of The Two Allies who have done
> much to reveal Calvin Coolidge into
> the Vice-Presidency.*

Then Calvin Coolidge led up the allies which
assured the victory. He set out to arouse the
will of the people without which law is not
law. In support of the Commissioner and for
the restoration of law and order and for the
reëstablishment of the police force, he issued
one order and two proclamations. He wired
Samuel Gompers two messages as straight as
electricity ever carried from a public official
to labor, adding those words now tattooed into
history:

> *"There is no right to strike against
> the public safety by anybody, any-
> where, any time."*

He set out to create and establish a public
sentiment behind the Commissioner which was

invaluable. It took root. It sprouted. The
opposition began to waver. The men who deserted their posts and left the city helpless were
not reinstated. Law and order was reëstablished and a practically new police force. It
was a great victory.

*The Commissioner and the Governor
each was vital to the other.*

There is no man in a position to estimate
more intelligently the Police Commissioner and
the Governor in their attitudes towards the police
strike than the Hon. Herbert Parker. No one
stood closer to the crisis than he. He is a former Attorney-General, now a lawyer in Boston,
brilliant, with a fine sense of honor. He has
always shown a vivid public spirit. His un-
qualified commendation of the Governor is
particularly significant because he was then
counsel to the Commissioner. He gave his ser-
vices. His compensation was simply nominal,
necessary for his qualification under the statute
as counsel. He says:

"The incidents of the so-called Police Strike
in the City of Boston, then engaging, as now
again engage the tense interest of the public.

The Transcript
THE GOVERNOR   THE POLICE COMMISSIONER
Render therefore unto the Caesars the things which are theirs

Issues of vital significance in the administration of Governor Coolidge pass in review. In the clearer light of passing time those qualities, which brought him at once into deserved and conspicuous national regard and admiration, are more distinctly revealed.

"The controversy need not now be renewed, which, at the time, found more or less intelligent expression in the public prints and in the hostile opinions of those whose sympathies were with the members of the police force who abandoned their duties; or of those who believed that credit for the ultimate vindication of the law, with the nation-wide recognition of its salutory and impressive influence and example, should be ascribed either to the Governor, Mr. Curtis, the Police Commissioner, or to others in political life.

"The Police Commissioner, by provision of law, is appointed by the Governor, and Mr. Curtis was so appointed by a predecessor of Governor Coolidge. His powers and duties, conferred and imposed by statute, made him solely responsible for the civil guardianship of the City of Boston as executive head of the Police Department. With the administration of his office no other authority could interfere, nor could he divide or share his responsibility with any other official of the City or State.

"Openly and defiantly members of the police force had violated a lawful order and regulation promulgated by the Commissioner, forbidding affiliation with outside organizations. The Commissioner proceeded in lawful course to enforce this regulation by formal trial of those who had violated its provisions. The obvious, inevitable, and expected adjudication of their guilt, excited a sympathetic breach of duty by their fellows, resulting in a secretly organized desertion of their posts, and the immediate, but brief outburst of lawlessness and violence, which, for a time, the remaining loyal police force was unable to wholly suppress. Supported by a universal approving sentiment of the people of the Commonwealth, the military forces of the State were immediately and lawfully called into service by the Mayor and the Governor, and instantly order was restored; and save for some isolated traces of a night of lawlessness, and the presence of militia men in the streets of Boston, the affairs of the City proceeded in normal course, while the depleted police force was in process of re-organization.

"The Governor did not intervene, prior to the exercise of his constitutional authority in calling the military arm of the public service into action, nor did he till then assume to in any wise advise or direct the Commissioner in the discharge of the duties of his own office as defined by the statute. The Commissioner was called upon to face, as he did, alone and with full realization of its grave issue, the emergency that confronted him. He knew that only through the unfaltering enforcement of the lawful requirements of the service that he had established and must control, could he maintain the efficiency or the vital morale of the police force in the maintenance of the law, and the protection of the city which he had sworn to preserve. Undeterred by threats, unaffected by solicitations and timorous suggestions of compromise with the offenders who had betrayed their trust, he maintained his steadfast course, universally approved by the people of the Commonwealth, who had discerned that the issue was the survival or destruction of the State itself.

"When, and perhaps when first he could intervene, the Governor did so, exercising his own supreme authority under the law, superceding the assumption by the Mayor of a supposed authority to take over command of the Police Department. The Governor directed the Commissioner to act only under such direction as the State executive might prescribe, and meanwhile to conduct his administration of the Police Department in accordance with his own vested authority, and thereafter no further order or direction was communicated by the Governor to the Commissioner.

"Thence forward, as before, Mr. Curtis directed and conducted the affairs of his office, exercised its every authority under the law in his own sound discretion, and in resolute performance of his duty. Had he faltered, had he, seduced or persuaded by insidious suggestions of compromise, yielded and given over the control of the city to those who had allied themselves with the evil doers who had betrayed their pledge of service and had sought to gain their own ends, by surrendering the city deprived of their protection to the terrors of the mob; had the Commissioner, in fear, or misled by the panic-stricken appeals of would-be advisers, opened the gates of the citadel to its invaders; upon what walls or towers could the Governor have raised the standard of the authority of the law, emblazoned with his own matchless phrases proclaiming its supremacy?

"There need be no discussion as to the comparative distinction in exalted public service between the Governor and the Police Commissioner. Without either the great issue would have passed, unrecognized, as one of the most momentous incidents in the history of the State or Nation.

"Mr. Curtis alone in the forefront of battle held his lines unbroken till victory was attained.

"The Governor, instantly responding to the call of a great occasion, which he at once perceived, with consummate sagacity, with courage and determination of supreme quality, marshalled all the forces of the Commonwealth to make the institutions of our law secure and impregnable for all time against further assault, by treachery or violence. No other chief magistrate has been gifted as he to touch and inspire by both appeal and command the patriotic faith of his people. Only his own faith, his sentiment and marvelous power of expression could

have stirred, as he did, the people of Massachusetts and the nation itself to a recognition and
renewal of their pledge and service to the tri-
umphant maintenance of our law, inviolate, un-
moved, whether assaulted by its enemies within
or without our borders.

"Vigilant, deliberate, with inflexible courage,
the chief magistrate suffered no incident of the
impending crisis to escape his forecasting consideration. He waited the just and appropriate
moment for his action, and then, with full force
of lawful authority and with overwhelming
weight of the people's will behind him, he struck,
and, with supreme mastery of the event, stood
revealed as a true leader of men, of patriotism,
courage and wisdom, proven through the trial of
faith and of conflict.

"He will meet, again, undaunted, with clear
vision and with the sure confidence of his coun-
trymen, the grave crises that may attend his de-
voted service in the highest field of endeavor
upon which man may enter, and to which he has
been called by the decree of tragic fate."

The Boston police strike of September, 1919,
made Calvin Coolidge known throughout the
country as the apostle of law and order. It gave
him an issue and an opportunity. It hurried

him into the Vice-Presidency. The importance
of this issue is fully recognized only by those
who lived in that city at that time, which, when
the police deserted their posts was open to the
possibilities of the mob. Boston only can understand that type of helplessness. Such an issue,
or any issue, history is only too quick to forget.
The risks of life dwarf as they pass backwards,
for joy that a man is born into the world. They
are greatest when faced. The English jockey as
he turns into the stretch before the crowds and
the cheers and the music, hanging over the
withers of his thoroughbred, forgets the hurdle
he has topped and fastens his eyes only on the
hurdle that is before him, which he seeks safely
to negotiate, and which alone stands between the
blue ribbon and himself.

The Boston police strike, its issue and its determination by the Police Commissioner and by
the Governor, ought to grow in realization and
recognition with each passing hour. It is significant that steps which had begun in other
parts of the country for the unionizing of the
police were then abandoned. The issue died.
It was a great issue. It was greatly met.

Render therefore unto the Caesars the
things which are theirs.

CHAPTER VIII

A Profile

"Seest thou a man diligent in his business, he shall stand before Kings."

THE country has probably never seen a man prominent in public life like him. No one thinks of opposing him and his great strength has come to him, he has not gone to it. He has never been known to make the usual moves towards political preferment. Most men impress one with trying to shape their own political fortunes, he appears indifferent. He has been content to rest his political hopes, if he has had any, on the political duties he has had to perform, however humble. The great reason for his political success is his own personality which appeals to one not for what it appears to be but for what it is. Unlike most politicians, he does not play a part, he is himself. He moves quietly and efficiently. He talks only when he has something to say but he listens respectfully whether there is something to hear

FOR BETTER FOR WORSE

or not. He has humor. He can make a pleasantry and enjoy a pleasantry but he does not
use humor only to make for others amusement
or for himself votes. A nod from him upon the
street is better than an ebullition from another
and even this is unnecessary for he is known to
be a democrat. He has come surely.

*He has uncommon sense. He is
always in preparation.*

In his first year in the Massachusetts House in
1907 he was not regarded as a leader because
he had not been in political life long enough to
be known. Things went after him. He did not
go after them. In his second year in the State
Senate in 1913, when he was Chairman of the
important Committee on Railroads, he was a
Chairman who presided; a man who made only
the necessary motions of mind, mouth or of
body. He never writes when he can talk, and he
never talks when he can nod. He was never
opposed, personally; he has no enemies in the
usual sense. Few men have fewer critics. He
had as intelligent and as detailed a knowledge
of the bills he had to pass on as any man in the
State House. He sees only one side of a ques-

tion, its merits. He has shown independence as
a legislator and

> *is as quick to stand by the weak when*
> *they are right as to leave power when*
> *it is wrong.*

He has had as little newspaper notice as any
man of his prominence. This has been because
he has avoided it. His speeches are unique and
strong for their thought and for their epigrammatic brevity. His political strength is largely
because the public have been curious to study
the personality of the only man of that kind
they have seen. The more of the man they
studied, the more of a man they found. He has
a maximum of business, a minimum of froth.
He has patience, tenacity, and self-control,
qualities which enable one to stand before
kings. As Lieutenant-Governor and as Vice-
President he was loyal to his Chiefs to a
degree too seldom found among his predecessors. His life has enabled him to know and to
understand all sorts of men, for he has been of
them. These men made him Governor, for they
liked him for his originality, his modesty, his
democracy and his ability. Most men are con-

tent to be honored by the office they seek. He
gives a dignity to the many high honors which
have seemed naturally to come to him. He is
more of an asset to public office than public
office is an asset to him. He is a character exceeded by none in interest for study, still incomplete, probably always incomplete. He has the
charm of mystery which puzzles and appeals.
When, pursuant to a fine tradition, in early
January 1919, the cannon upon the Common
proclaimed to the people of Massachusetts that
the hills of her sister State, Vermont, had given
them a chief executive, those who would learn
to live knew that merit and fortune sometimes
walk hand in hand and that the Commonwealth
had again the sort of Governor she ought to
have, measuring up to her high ideals.

An issue hurried him into the Vice-Presidency.
Greater responsibilities stimulate further analysis. He is a student of political economy. As
a servant of the people he is as careful of his
official as he is of his personal expenditures.
To him the public and the private pocket in this
way are the same. He is a student of philosophy.

He is led by logic and not by emotion,
by fidelity and not by ambition.

He supplements leadership with coöperation. He sets his compass not only for today but also for tomorrow and for a course beyond the line of the horizon. Those who study him, know him, turn to him, rely on him. They, only, know him, for his virtues he does not radio. The people see in him one of their own. The powerful turn to him because he is an intellectual aristocrat and the weak because he is also a plain farmer. He is one of them all. He met the great issue, law and order. He recognizes that law is but the will of the people which he successfully sets out to arouse. He has the strength of a deep running river, powerful and placid. He has an inset religious faith.

Of such is Calvin Coolidge. He has made his five talents ten. Providence has led him on, made strong allies his handmaidens, made his path straight. Law and order revealed him into the Vice-Presidency.

He now holds the highest office on earth by virtue of a title greater than that of any electorate. God made him President.

CHAPTER IX

ALONG THE POTOMAC

*"God moves in a mysterious way,
His wonders to perform."*

PARTICULARLY because of the issue, law and order, it was natural that when the Presidential storm of 1920 broke and men were named for the Republican Presidential nomination, the Governor was among them. Significantly, however, some of the Republican leaders of his own State sulked in their tents. They were then without a gift of prophecy which they now lament. A determined effort was made to secure for Leonard Wood the Massachusetts delegation. The Governor, however, continued with his duties in his own way, unrippled. When asked if he were a candidate for the Presidency, he said:

"I am not a candidate for the Presidency. I am Governor of Massachusetts and am content to do my only duty, the day's work as such."

101

Again, in a characteristic whimsical vein, he said: "If you are asked if I am a candidate for the Presidency, tell the truth."

Coolidge had been reëlected Governor in the fall of 1919 on the issue of law and order by the greatest vote to that time cast, which was before women voted. In the spirit of these statements he finished the old term and began the new. In the Republican State Convention of 1919, strangely, there was some discussion over the plank on The League of Nations, then the great issue. The matter was compromised in a way which met with satisfaction. The party however, should have stood without hesitation to the letter logically behind Senator Lodge and his position because his record was the party record. He was the party. He had made it what it was, whether it was good, whether it was bad.

The Coolidge sentiment for President in the spring of 1920 began to grow. He, however, did nothing to encourage it. It was not his way. He was content to do the day's work.

Headquarters which ardent friends had opened for him in Washington he closed.

He was content to drift along in the Coolidge current which he had always found to be a strong tide. He knew that he lay in an advantageous position on the political beach, to be washed safely high on the shore. He knew that his cause was strongest as an harmonizing suggestion should the convention fail to nominate, otherwise. His cause was thus unscarred by contest. It was his way. His book, "Have Faith in Massachusetts," was widely circulated by his friends throughout the country by which he became better known. The story is told that a young woman went into an ill-equipped country store in Berkshire County and asked: "Have you faith in Massachusetts?" The answer was "Yes" and "No."

A notable delegation, in quality if not in quantity, went to Chicago in June for Coolidge. They had taken the bits into their own mouths and would not be controlled by him. Notable among them were then Lieutenant-Governor Channing Cox, then Speaker Joseph Everett Warner and the Hon. Benjamin Loring Young, then reconciled to political preferment. Although they recognized that advancement for Coolidge and his retirement as Governor meant

probable advancement for them, this did not
palsy their hands or chill the inside of their
footgear. No one at Chicago was more eloquent for Calvin Coolidge than they.

*Their devotion and self-effacement is
one of the most touching and noblest
pages in the political history of the
Commonwealth.*

There were others. The Hon. Charles L.
Burrill is a man of independence and vigor. He
is not in need of a tonic. When he is with you,
he is with you. He is now a Councillor, then
State Treasurer. He has a creditable public
record. Thomas W. White was a legislative colleague of Coolidge. Tom knew him. Coolidge
had made him Supervisor of Administration, the
most important office in the State House. White
is a politician. A splendid quality of his as
such is that he recognizes the obligation of reci-
procity. This he cheerfully then did. William
F. Whiting of Holyoke is a member of a family
distinguished as manufacturers. These names
stand high on the roll of honor of those loyal to
Calvin Coolidge, not alone in 1923 when it is

easy, but particularly in 1920, when it was not
so easy.

Louis K. Liggett, a successful, respected man-
ufacturer and retailer of drugs in Boston, was
another leader in the Coolidge delegation. In
his zeal, the story is told, that he invaded even
the boudoir of the Senior Senator from Massachusetts, when the clock had fought its course
half-way from caviar to shredded wheat, seeking to enlist him in his army. A Cabot was
actually in bed. A Cabot never goes to bed
except perhaps furtively outside of Suffolk and
Essex Counties. He retires. "Senator," cried he,
when he had hardly closed the door, removed his
hat and gums, and a Cabot turning, had faced
him, "Calvin Coolidge is the greatest man in
this country since the days of Abraham Lincoln." The Senior Senator made an effort to
control himself long enough to reply: "Will you
kindly repeat, that is, the fifth word?" When
Henry Cabot Lodge had satisfied himself that
he had again heard the word, "greatest," he
turned languidly on his right side, facing the
wall, and reached for a soothing powder. His
forefinger hesitated at the push button which
hung over the bed to plunge the room in dark-

ness only because of the obligation of a host, to
which a Cabot could not be dead.   Calvin
Coolidge was placed before the convention for
President by the Speaker of the House, the Hon.
Frederick Huntington Gillett.   He is a son of
Westfield, loyal to Calvin Coolidge, not only
now but also then, and of the Connecticut River
Valley, though well up on its western banks
beyond the reach of its highest tides.   The nomination was seconded by Mrs. Alexandra Car-
lisle in an eloquent speech.   Women then made
their political debut in her.   On the first ballot,
Coolidge received 34 votes, including 1 from
Kentucky, 2 from New York, 2 from South
Carolina, 1 from Texas and 28 of the 35 Massachusetts delegates.   Massachusetts had been
hammered hard for Leonard Wood for six
months.   Coolidge had done nothing, and his
adherents had been strangled by him so far as
he was able to do so.   And yet, seven only faltered.   Curiously, Vermont's 8 votes went to
Leonard Wood for President but for Coolidge
for Vice-President, on the first ballots.

The Governor was nominated for the Vice-
Presidency at Chicago, June 12, 1920, late in
the afternoon by the Hon. Wallace McCamant of

Portland, Oregon.   It was enough to mention his
name to the convention and it swept with a spon-
taneity unexcelled in history.   When the news
came to him at The Adams House in Boston,
where he was then living as Governor, he stood
at the telephone.   He turned to his wife and
said, simply:

"Nominated."

He was as much Coolidge as when he heard that
he had been first politically uncrated and elected
a Councilman in Northampton in 1899.   His
wife, Grace Goodhue Coolidge, could, would
and did betray human joy.   The humblest serf
of the hotel, as he hurried up purely Volstedian
beverages to his adherents, was more exuberant
than the Governor and quicker to betray it.
Frank Stearns, who always aimed at the stars
for Coolidge, looked upon the Vice-Presidency
as a bauble.   He contemplated retiring into a
monastery.   Coolidge was formally notified of
his nomination at Northampton, July 27, 1920.
On that day, Senator Crane, one of the Governor's most sympathetic allies, showed signs of
his final illness.   He was loved because he lived:
"It is more blessed to give than to receive."

He gave to those in trouble freely of his money but more than this freely of his time. No politician was closer to Calvin Coolidge than

> *Murray Crane, who drew all men to
> him with hooks of steel.*

To his place, the Hon. William M. Butler has now succeeded. He stood closest to Crane. He has won the respect of the people by his foresight and thrift.

In the campaign which then began the Governor made a number of political speeches throughout the country which were of great value to the ticket, although he was handicapped by his onerous duties as Governor. These he carefully prepared, for no one is less given than he to extempore speaking. These speeches he wrote out in long hand before they were typed, as he does with all his speeches. Coolidge particularly appealed among the farmers of the West, for he had always been a farmer himself. When he saw a plough, he knew it. In November, the ticket was elected by the greatest plurality known in history.

January and February 1921 were welcome days of comparative rest for Calvin Coolidge.

He had retired as Governor and had returned to "The Executive Mansion" in Northampton. There with his wife, and the boys at study in the public schools of the town, he was happier than he had been for years or was to be, for he likes simplicity and the opportunity for study. For the first time since the year 1909, the year between his service as Representative and as Mayor, he was in private life. He had become the most distinguished son of the Connecticut River Valley in its history.

Coolidge found much correspondence to keep him busy and he was preparing for his duties in the United States Senate as he always prepared. The letters which came into Northampton for him, and the post office became a busy one, were longer naturally than those that went out. The incoming and not the outgoing was the big mail. To one loyal friend, then under attack, who wrote him a real letter, congratulating the country on his elevation, Coolidge wrote simply:

"Thanks. Matt. 5:10, 11. C. C."

He was never in finer form as Calvin the Silent, for he denied the letter even a date. On August 3, 1923, this letter was framed and deposited in a safe deposit vault, and not in a trunk, backed, "Correspondence, Calvin Coolidge." Strangely, some few critics look upon a man who has twice been President of the Massachusetts Senate, three times Lieutenant-Governor, and twice Governor, with suspicion. They suggest in substance that in politics, in stature, he is a Tom Thumb, and in his success, a casualty.

Massachusetts is a fairly intelligent State and is not in the habit of digesting for seven long years a peppered chocolate.

On March 4, 1921, Coolidge became Vice-President and by virtue of his office presided over the Senate of the United States. He was then forty-eight years old, one year for each star in the flag. The seat in which he sat quietly, Roosevelt had writhed in. Strangely, he had turned from swinging the gavel over the Massachusetts Senate and the Hon. George Bosworth Churchill, also a great son of Amherst, to that of maintaining order over her great sister and Hiram Johnson. The Presidency has saved him from Magnus. He was asked to sit in the Cabinet of the President. He was the first Vice-

THE THREE COOLIDGE MEN. WASHINGTON

Calvin Coolidge, Jr.   The President   John Coolidge

President to face a proposition of this delicacy, for The White House and The Senate had not always been a symbol of sympathetic communion. This he did with great tact and profit to the country then and later.

He lived with his wife at The New Willard and with his boys when they were not at school or at the top of the Washington Monument. He pursued his duties quietly and efficiently as always nor did he immediately seek to ally himself with a press agency or subscribe to a clipping bureau. It is not his first hope for the day, that of most public servants restless for advance, to read about himself, praise or even condemnation. There is no easier way to jeopardize an appetite for breakfast. He also faced other hurdles, harder for one of his tastes if this word may be properly used, the continuous dinners which the Vice-President is paid his salary to eat. Fortunately, The New Willard is maintained on the European plan. Calvin paid for what he ate only, and more than this he ate what he paid for. Entertained often at luncheon at noon by some Senator who hoped to be recognized by The Chair later in the day and dining at some Embassy in the evening, Calvin's board

bill at the hotel could have easily been paid by
a parish priest. It is a matter of regret though
not of surprise to those who know our hero,
that, whether he ate much or ate little, he ate
more than he talked but less than he listened.

At one of these dinners, a Washington matron
sat beside him. She established herself then
and there as a *raconteur* of high order for there
also sat beside her Herbert Hoover. Hers was
an admirable background against which she was
set off. Her heart set on the biggest game within
her reach, she forgot the man who fed the Bel-
gians and concentrated her ingenuity on Calvin,
to tempt him to speak. He was noticed address-
ing her almost excitedly. When later she was
asked for the cause of her great triumph, she
replied:

*"I did not make much progress with
him until I reached the Northampton
post office."*

Here again this little anecdote is significant,
for Coolidge is preoccupied always with great
questions and when he found that he could work
his mouth and rest his mind on a familiar theme,
then he was ready to coöperate and happy.

A prominent man in Washington, a good judge
of men and a loyal friend of the President, says:
"I like him because I don't know why I like
him; because he don't seem to care whether I
like him or not; because he's the only one of
his species, which I didn't know existed; because he's not like other politicians, doesn't
give away cigars, kiss other babies than his own
or tell entertaining stories; because he gets by
on merit, not personal charm, because to him a
political job is a business opportunity; because,
in easy English, he F. O. B's the freight."

Of such was the life of Calvin Coolidge in
Washington.   More than this, when he was not
there or at home on the farm, he was speaking
for the administration throughout the country.

No one exceeded him in his loyalty to
Warren Harding and his administra-
tion.

At midnight after the day of August 2, a
motor and messengers hurried over the rough
road from Ludlow to Plymouth. They carried
a message of great sorrow and of high responsibility. The President was dead. In a white
cottage close by the highway, Calvin Coolidge

slept. From peace and simplicity and the homely duties and pleasures about the farm, he was aroused to face the high office of President. No man has passed through a greater transition than that of the loyal aide-de-camp and friend of Warren Gamaliel Harding.

> *Never has greater distinction and greater power come to any one among more simple surroundings. It is a symbol of the democracy of American institutions which will always live in American history, that opportunity and honor are open to all.*

The little white cottage will never die. It staged a drama which will forever thrill every American citizen, from the powerful to the ploughman.

In his great hour, Calvin Coolidge thought first of his father. It was he who as Notary Public administered to his son the oath of office at seventeen minutes of three in the morning, eastern standard time, in these words: "I, Calvin Coolidge, do solemnly swear that I will faithfully execute the office of President of the United States, and that I will, to the best of

THE PLACE OF THE ACCESSION. JOHN C. COOLIDGE HOUSE

The President and Mrs. Coolidge in foreground

my ability, preserve, protect and defend the constitution of the United States. So help me God." The only other words said were by the President: "Grace, get another lamp." And there was light. Calvin Coolidge became President of the United States. When the great test came, official and personal, he showed the stoicism of an Indian. He was himself.

In his first words to the American people, the President said:

"Reports have reached me, which I fear are correct, that President Harding is gone. The world has lost a great and good man. I mourn his loss. He was my chief and my friend. It will be my purpose to carry out the policies which he has begun for the service of the American people and for meeting their responsibilities wherever they may arise. For this purpose I shall seek the coöperation of all those who have been associated with the President during his term of office. Those who have given their efforts to assist him, I wish to remain in office, that they may assist me. I have faith that God will direct the destinies of our nation."

In his first act as President, he stood alone at his mother's grave in Plymouth, for which he halted his progress to Washington. He was true to those scriptural words, the only commandment with promise:

"Honour thy father and mother."

Mention is now reserved here for one who is now dead, on August 2, 1923, and who by his characteristic, kindly and wise foresight did much to adapt at the Cabinet table Calvin Coolidge for his responsibilities as President.

Warren Harding as a man was a Christian gentleman. His was a faith which comprehended all, Protestant and Catholic, Gentile and Jew, who recognized in him a spiritual aristocrat. In his death the people forgot the President for the man, for his personal charm could not be augmented by the splendor of any office, even the high one which he held. This they showed at his death in expressions of sorrow and respect unprecedented, marked first by silence and second by numbers, the great and the small, the young and the old, the strong and the weak. His Christian qualities are best shown upon the walls of *The Marion Star* by this, his newspaper creed:

"Remember there are two sides to every

question. Get both. Be truthful. Get the facts. Mistakes are inevitable, but strive for accuracy. I would rather have one story exactly right than a hundred half wrong. Be decent. Be fair. Be generous. Boost—don't knock. There's good in everybody. Bring out the good in everybody, and never needlessly hurt the feeling of anybody. In reporting a political gathering, get the facts, tell the story as it is, not as you would like to have it. Treat all parties alike. If there's any politics to be played, we will play it in our editorial columns. Treat all religious matter reverently. If it can possibly be avoided, never bring ignominy to an innocent woman or child in telling of the misdeeds or misfortune of a relative. Don't wait to be asked, but do it without the asking.

And above all be clean. Never let a dirty word or suggestive story get into type. I want this paper so conducted that it can go into any home without destroying the innocence of any child."

Warren Harding as President remembered his country. He forgot himself and his own life. He lost his life. He has found it. He fore-

saw the stake which he did not seek to evade,
for he was not in sound physical condition.   He
was a patriot.   He came into the office of President at a period trying for the country, trying
for him.   It was a period of reconstruction,
restlessness, when the people were impatient and
quick in comment and criticism.   He was led,
not by ambition, but by duty.   He had a kindly
heart and an unwillingness to pain.   He had
sound sense.   He had courage.   He had fidelity.
He did not shrink from bristling issues even
where the leaders of his own party were divided.
He was insistent for the enforcement of the law
and the respect of the constitution.   The Dis-
armament Conference for the peace of the
world, called by him, was his first great hope.
He will live in history not only as a great Peace
President, none greater, but more than this as a
Christian gentleman.

> *"The strenuous day is past,*
> *The march, the fight.*
> *The bugle sounds at last:*
> *Lights out.   Good night."*

Warren Harding is dead.   The Presidency of
the United States, no higher, more honorable or

more powerful office on earth, never dies. Calvin Coolidge succeeds to the command.

"Close up the ranks.   March on."

To the people of the United States remains the high duty:

Have faith in Calvin Coolidge.

CHAPTER X

Some High Tides

*"Let reverence of the law be
breathed by every mother to the
lisping babe that prattles on her lap;
let it be taught in schools, seminaries
and colleges; let it be written in
primers, spelling books and alma-
nacs; let it be preached from pulpits
and proclaimed in legislative halls
and enforced in courts of justice; let
it become the political religion
of the nation."—Lincoln.*

On the Power of Religion
C. C.

"It was because religion gave the people a
new importance and a new glory that they
demanded a new freedom and a new Government. We cannot in our generation reject the
cause and retain the result. If the institutions
they adopted are to survive, if the Government
which they founded is to endure, it will be

because the people continue to have similar religious beliefs. It is idle to discuss freedom and equality on any other basis. It is useless to expect substantial reforms from any other motive. They cannot be administered from without. They must come from within."

On the American Revolution
'94–'95—C. C.

"When history looks beyond the immediate causes of the American Revolution for the justifying principles, it is very soon brought back to the spirit of English liberty. It is the same genius for freedom that has led the race from the primeval forests of Germany to the thirteenth amendment to the constitution.

"Such an honorable antiquity of political ideas has made the race very conservative of self-government. The idea is prehistoric. . . . Although it is characteristic of Englishmen to have great love for a king so long as he respects the liberties of the people, yet the fact that they drove out one king; rebelled against two; and executed three shows clearly enough that there was always a strong idea of the divine right of the people as well as of kings. Precedents, then, are by no means wanting among Englishmen for the successful resistance of arbitrary despotism whenever it encroached upon their liberties.

"Another fact that must be noted is the character of the colonists, and especially those of Massachusetts. These were the Puritans who had fought the wars of liberty in England. . . . Of all the race they were the most tenacious of their rights and the most jealous of their liberties.

"The American Revolution was not, then, any struggle for emancipation from slavery; the colonists were free men. Nor was it at first so much for gaining new liberties as preserving the old. Nor can it, as is often thought, be called a war between different nations.

"Both sides were Englishmen who gloried in the name of England. . . . The ablest advocates of the colonial cause were members of Parliament, while the most ardent advocates of the king were colonists. The real object of resistance was to gain security from parliamentary encroachments. This was the chief cause for which the revolutionists contended, but by no means all they attained . . . the war was a

struggle for the retention of those institutions
that check oppression and violence.

"The colonists were . . . struggling to
change the foundation of government from
force to equality. . . . Great Britain had re-
course to acts of coercion. . . . Free government was destroyed. . . . Town meetings were
forbidden. . . . The form of government that
was thrust on Massachusetts was despotism such
as Englishmen would not have endured, even
in the days of Henry VIII.

"Though the injustice of taxation without
representation made a good war cry . . . it
is, in the last analysis, a dangerous principle.
. . . The fact is, it is a duty to the State to
pay taxes, and it is equally a duty to vote. It
does not follow that because the State requires
one duty it shall require the other.

"It cannot be, then, that the American Revolution was fought that colonists might escape
paying taxes. . . . The real principle was
not one of the right of the State or the duty of
citizens. It was a question of government, a
question of form and method. . . . It was not
so much a revolution, a propagation of new
ideas, as the maintenance of the old forms of

a representative government, of chartered rights and constitutional liberty. England had fought for this in 1688, and imagined it was secured. But it was only so in name. . . .

"Sovereignty is always finally vested in the people. . . . England had asserted it against the Stuarts, but George III forgot it. . . . The colonies were driven to assert by war what the Commons of England partially gained by legislation sixty years later. There was further gained in the United States a recognition that quality, not quantity, is the basis of the peerage of man, and accordingly all men were declared free and equal.

"Still there is another factor that must inevitably have led to separation. The great land of America had a part to play in the history of the world that could best be performed by making it an independent nation. England's great work was to plant colonies. America could not aid in that work. It was her place to found a great nation on this side of the Atlantic and to bring out the conception of free government. And when this was done, then America stretched out her hand over the sea to aid the oppressed of Europe, to furnish them a place of refuge, and, as soon as they could assume the duties, make them citizens, not alone of our United States, but of the world."

On Wit

Grove Oration — Amherst College — June, 1895, by "J. Calvin Coolidge"

"The mantle of truth falls upon the Grove Orator on condition he wear it wrong side out. For the Grove Oration is intended to give a glimpse of the only true side of college life — the inside. And how can this be displayed but by turning things wrong side out? That is the grove prerogative. We came out of doors to have plenty of room. Reconstructed Amherst has not yet decreed that 'fools may not speak wisely what wise men do foolishly.' Yet let no one expect that this is an occasion for feeding the multitude — on small fishes. I only bring the impressions that we gather by the way, whether they be pleasant as the breath of society roses from over the meadows of Old Hadley, or disagreeable as the ancient odors that filled Athenae Hall.

"Now college life has three relations — the

relation to the class, the relation to the faculty,
and the relation to other things. The class
relation begins with a cane rush where the
undergraduates use Anglo-Saxon, and ends with
a diploma where the faculty use Latin — if it
does not end before by a communication from
the President in just plain English. When we
had our first rush the streets of Amherst were
lit with matches. We lost the rush, but we
found our class spirit. Those were the days
when we looked with envy at even Professor
Charlie, and cooled our fevered brows at the
college well. Let memory draw us back once
more to the college well! Deep as the wily
schemes of 'Sleuth' Jaggar, the crafty man,
cool as the impudence of 'Jeff' Davis, refresh-
ing as the sparkling wit of 'Chipmunk' Hardy!
The freshman's first love! Many a man goes
home when he finds the college well is not dug
in Northampton.

"But sophomore year came at last. Probably
nearly every one would maintain that the only
proper thing to do when one comes to a description of sophomore year is to let the voice fall,
count four, and begin some other subject. In
fact, I have always been inclined to believe that

some impecunious sophomore, who may have
enticed him into buying a book on ornithology
or some kindred subject, first led Horace
Greeley to classify college men as horned cattle.

"But the great editor was a poor naturalist,
for even horned cattle would never try to steal
a railroad restaurant. Still we have to excuse
the sophomore worm, for he comes out of his
vacation cocoon a junior butterfly. Probably
it is better to be a junior than not to be. He
is the incarnation of all the attributes of a
college man. The plug hat is his. He goes
about 'seeking the bubble reputation even in
his own mouth.' Only last Decoration Day,
Lockwood delivered two addresses before people. The only trouble with junior year is that
it leaves one a senior. He needs no description.
You have all been looking at him for the last
week. Here are some living pictures representing the senior in repose.

"There is connected with our Christian College
an institution of most honorable antiquity called
a faculty. Some of its members, like comets
with long hair, move in orbits of enormous
eccentricity. Some seem but satellites revolving
around that 'tenebrific star' that 'did ray out

darkness' over the Amherst system. 'All the world's a stage, . . . all men . . . merely players . . . and one man in his time plays many parts.' But there are others. At the head of one of the best departments in College is Professor Frink. One man in the class allowed him to be mentioned on several pages of our *Olio*. That man had to send his regrets to the class supper from a distant city. But still the professor was not satisfied with our production, and even expressed himself in terms that were derogatory to its literary merit. It has been said that DeQuincey was a creature of the intellect. But though we would refuse to offer the excuse of Mother Eve that this serpent beguiled us, still the Board and the class behind it is willing to fall back upon the excuse of the late Adam that this woman gave to us and we did eat. He has indeed furnished us with fruit. There is a four years' course, too, under Dr. Hitchcock. 'The poor ye have always with you.' But not feeling at liberty to make use of the choice indecencies that are always so prevalent in the remarks of the venerable tarrier, it is necessary to refer him to Mr. Kelley. Was he the only member of the

faculty that was eminently fitted to hear Egan's
apology for talking *French* at the sophomore
supper, or had Egan infringed upon the domain
of the physical department?   I recommend the
Olio Board to compile statistics showing the
original sources of Dr. Tuttle's stories, and the
number of times he uses his favorite phrase
the 'piercèd hand.'   There are some who argue
that what the good Doctor took for a call to
the pulpit was in reality some other noise.   But
your grove orator does not think so, though it
may have been a subjective sensation.   The only
professor who seems positively disappointed
when a man does not flunk is Professor Wood.
But some men do disappoint him.   To a man
standing at the back of his class it must resemble
the circuit races.   Then there is the new labora-
tory, where Professor Harris delights to lecture
upon various, diverse, promiscuous and other
oratorical subjects, except chemistry.   He has
a lecture on the faculty in two sub-divisions
— Christians and gorillas — that actually sur-
passes the ordinary effort of a superintendent of
schools.   To a man who does not take geology
Professor Emerson looks like a kind old gentleman with a little of the good free wool

growing on his countenance; but the combined vocabularies of Kingsland and Sampson could not express the mind of a man trying to make up a cut in that department. Professor Neill seems to be trying to color himself with nicotine like a meerschaum pipe. He has partially succeeded with his whiskers. To attain perfection he needs to send himself away, and get himself boiled. Then if he came back at all he would come back a nice dark brown. But these are only a few snapshots from the side lines. In such departments as calculus, history, philosophy and many others, are men who teach. It is such men that have made Amherst what it is. I believe every Amherst man may point with pride at our faculty.

"I have said that there are other things. One of these is the town. It is largely made up of beautiful scenery and a kindly regard for a college man's money. But not so with all the townspeople. James Davis deserves a word of commendation, but I cannot give it to him, because he sent me word that whenever he was mentioned in this connection his wife made home life a misery to him. It seemed also at the opening of the year as if it would be neces-

sary to mention THE STUDENT, but ever since
Editor Law came back from Christmas vacation, wearing an engagement smile, and hum-
ming some ditty about 'over the river,' the
organ has taken a more readable standard. But
I cannot leave out the other classes. The fresh-
men still have more links than golf suits in
spite of the fact that Henry Clews may be
afflicted with only the eccentricities of genius.
The less one says about the sophomores, of
course the better one describes them. The
juniors have some musicians and little Johnnie
Pratt for a football captain.

"GENTLEMEN OF THE CLASS OF '95: Oh! you
need not look so alarmed. I am not going to
work off any song and dance about the cold,
cruel world. It may not be such a misfortune
to be out of college. It is not positive proof
that a diploma is a wolf because it comes to
you in sheep's clothing. No one in business
will have to pay Professor Tyler, him of the
nest-egg pate, two dollars for an extra examination. Of course we are not all stars. Post,
like the man in the moon, seems to have come
too soon to find his way to knowledge. Compton
has sometimes been unfortunate — when he

could not read between the lines. And there is
Charlie Little in his own specialty of drawing
himself into his shell like a turtle to exist solely
to and for self. In looking over the class book,
I see that the statistics committee made the mis-
take of not taking the opinion of the class to
see, whether, from present indications, Fiske's
failure to make the commencement stage was
due more to subjective causes than to objective
obstacles. But we have also such men as Colby,
who, at Chicago, sacrificed the brightest athletic
prospects of any man in the class for the sake
of Amherst, and every man in college knows
what reward he had for his loyalty. Wherever
we go, whatever we are, scientific or classical,
conditioned or unconditioned, degreed or dis-
agreed, we are going to be Amherst men. And
whoever sees a purple and white button marked
with '95 shall see the emblem of a class spirit
that will say, 'Old Amherst, doubtless always
right, but right or wrong, Old Amherst!' "

On Political Philosophy

First Inaugural
Massachusetts Senate, 1914
C. C.

"Honorable Senators:— I thank you —
with gratitude for the high honor given, with
appreciation for the solemn obligations assumed
— I thank you.

"This Commonwealth is one. We are all members of one body. The welfare of the weakest
and the welfare of the most powerful are insep-
arably bound together. Industry cannot flourish
if labor languish. Transportation cannot pros-
per if manufactures decline. The general welfare cannot be provided for in any one act, but
it is well to remember that the benefit of one is
the benefit of all, and the neglect of one is the
neglect of all. The suspension of one man's
dividends is the suspension of another man's
pay envelope.

"Men do not make laws. They do but discover them. Laws must be justified by something
more than the will of the majority. They must
rest on the eternal foundation of righteousness.
That state is most fortunate in its form of government which has the aptest instruments for

the discovery of laws. The latest, most modern, and nearest perfect system that statesmanship has devised is representative government. Its weakness is the weakness of us imperfect human beings who administer it. Its strength is that even such administration secures to the people more blessings than any other system ever produced. No nation has discarded it and retained liberty. Representative government must be preserved.

"Courts are established, not to determine the popularity of a cause, but to adjudicate and enforce rights. No litigant should be required to submit his case to the hazard and expense of a political campaign. No judge should be required to seek or receive political rewards. The courts of Massachusetts are known and honored wherever men love justice. Let their glory suffer no diminution at our hands. The electorate and judiciary cannot combine. A hearing means a hearing. When the trial of causes goes outside the court-room, Anglo-Saxon constitutional government ends.

"The people cannot look to legislation generally for success. Industry, thrift, character, are not conferred by act or resolve. Govern-

ment cannot relieve from toil. It can provide no
substitute for the rewards of service. It can,
of course, care for the defective and recognize
distinguished merit. The normal must care for
themselves. Self-government means self-support.

"Man is born into the universe with a personality that is his own. He has a right that is
founded upon the constitution of the universe
to have property that is his own. Ultimately,
property rights and personal rights are the same
thing. The one cannot be preserved if the other
be violated. Each man is entitled to his rights
and the rewards of his service be they never so
large or never so small.

"History reveals no civilized people among
whom there were not a highly educated class,
and large aggregations of wealth, represented
usually by the clergy and the nobility. Inspiration has always come from above. Diffusion
of learning has come down from the university
to the common school — the kindergarten is
last. No one would now expect to aid the common school by abolishing higher education.

"It may be that the diffusion of wealth works
in an analogous way. As the little red schoolhouse is builded in the college, it may be that

the fostering and protection of large aggregations of wealth are the only foundation on
which to build the prosperity of the whole people. Large profits mean large pay rolls. But
profits must be the result of service performed.
In no land are there so many and such large
aggregations of wealth as here; in no land do
they perform larger service; in no land will the
work of a day bring so large a reward in material and spiritual welfare.

"Have faith in Massachusetts. In some unim-
portant detail some other States may surpass
her, but in the general results, there is no place
on earth where the people secure, in a larger
measure, the blessings of organized government,
and nowhere can those functions more properly
be termed self-government.

"Do the day's work. If it be to protect the
rights of the weak, whoever objects, do it. If it
be to help a powerful corporation better to serve
the people, whatever the opposition, do that.
Expect to be called a stand-patter, but don't be
a stand-patter. Expect to be called a demagogue, but don't be a demagogue. Don't hesitate to be as revolutionary as science. Don't
hesitate to be as reactionary as the multiplica-

tion table. Don't expect to build up the weak by
pulling down the strong. Don't hurry to legis-
late. Give administration a chance to catch up
with legislation.

"We need a broader, firmer, deeper faith in
the people — a faith that men desire to do right,
that the Commonwealth is founded upon a righteousness which will endure, a reconstructed
faith that the final approval of the people is
given not to demagogues, slavishly pandering to
their selfishness, merchandising with the clamor
of the hour, but to statesmen, ministering to
their welfare, representing their deep, silent,
abiding convictions.

"Statutes must appeal to more than material
welfare. Wages won't satisfy, be they never so
large. Nor houses; nor lands; nor coupons,
though they fall thick as the leaves of autumn.
Man has a spiritual nature. Touch it, and it
must respond as the magnet responds to the
pole. To that, not to selfishness, let the laws of
the Commonwealth appeal. Recognize the
immortal worth and dignity of man. Let the
laws of Massachusetts proclaim to her humblest
citizen, performing the most menial task, the
recognition of his manhood, the recognition that

all men are peers, the humblest with the most exalted, the recognition that all work is glorified. Such is the path to equality before the law. Such is the foundation of liberty under the law. Such is the sublime revelation of man's relation to man — Democracy."

SECOND INAUGURAL
MASSACHUSETTS SENATE, 1915
C. C.
[Shortest inaugural in history.]

"HONORABLE SENATORS: — My sincerest thanks, I offer you. Conserve the firm foundations of our institutions. Do your work with the spirit of a soldier in the public service. Be loyal to the Commonwealth and to yourselves. And be brief; above all things,
Be Brief."

ON LAW AND ORDER

THE POLICE STRIKE

"*The Commonwealth of Massachusetts
By His Excellency Calvin Coolidge, Governor*

"A PROCLAMATION
"The entire State Guard of Massachusetts has

been called out.   Under the Constitution the
Governor is the Commander-in-Chief thereof by
an authority of which he could not if he chose
divest himself.   That command I must and will
exercise.   Under the law I hereby call on all
the police of Boston who have loyally and in
a never-to-be-forgotten way remained on duty
to aid me in the performance of my duty of
the restoration and maintenance of order in the
city of Boston, and each of such officers is
required to act in obedience to such orders as
I may hereafter issue or cause to be issued.

"I call on every citizen to aid me in the
maintenance of law and order.

"Given at the Executive Chamber, in Boston,
this eleventh day of September, in the year of
our Lord one thousand nine hundred and nineteen, and of the Independence of the United
States of America the one hundred and forty-
fourth.

CALVIN COOLIDGE.

"By His Excellency the Governor,
     ALBERT P. LANGTRY
Secretary of the Commonwealth

God save the Commonwealth of Massachusetts."

"AN ORDER

Boston, September 11, 1919

"To EDWIN U. CURTIS,
As you are Police Commissioner of the City of Boston,

Executive Order No. 1

"You are hereby directed, for the purpose of assisting me in the performance of my duty, pursuant to the proclamation issued by me this day, to proceed in the performance of your duties as Police Commissioner of the City of Boston under my command and in obedience to such orders as I shall issue from time to time, and obey only such orders as I may so issue or transmit.

CALVIN COOLIDGE
Governor of Massachusetts."

(The only literature, of this sort,
        in political history.)

(Copy)

WESTERN UNION TELEGRAM

September 13, 1919.

Mr. Samuel Gompers, President,
    American Federation of Labor,
        New York City, N. Y.

Under the law the suggestions contained in
your telegram are not within the authority of
the Governor of Massachusetts but only of the
Commissioner of Police of the city of Boston.
With the maintenance of discipline in his department I have no authority to interfere. He
has decided that the men here abandoned their
sworn duty and has accordingly declared their
places vacant. I shall support the Commissioner
in the execution of law and maintenance of
order.

CALVIN COOLIDGE, *Governor.*

WESTERN UNION TELEGRAM

(Copy)

Sunday, September 14, 1919.

Mr. Samuel Gompers, President,
   American Federation of Labor,
   New York City, N. Y.

Replying to your telegram. I have already refused to remove the Police Commissioner of Boston. I did not appoint him. He can assume no position which the Courts would uphold except what the people have by the authority of their law vested in him. He speaks only with their voice. The right of the police of Boston to affiliate has always been questioned, never granted, is now prohibited. The suggestion of President Wilson to Washington does not apply to Boston. There the police have remained on duty. Here the Policemen's Union left their duty, an action which President Wilson characterized as a crime against civilization. Your assertion that the Commissioner was wrong cannot justify the wrong of leaving the city unguarded. That furnished the opportunity, the criminal element furnished the action. There

is no right to strike against the public safety
by anybody, anywhere, any time. You ask that
the public safety again be placed in the hands
of these same policemen while they continue
in disobedience to the laws of Massachusetts
and in their refusal to obey the orders of the
Police Department. Nineteen men have been
tried and removed. Others having abandoned
their duty their places have under the law been
declared vacant in the opinion of the Attorney
General. I can suggest no authority outside
the Courts to take further action. I wish to
join and assist in taking a broad view of every
situation. A grave responsibility rests on all
of us. You can depend on me to support you
in every legal action and sound policy. I am
equally determined to defend the sovereignty
of Massachusetts and to maintain the authority
and jurisdiction over her public officers where
it has been placed by the Constitution and Laws
of her people.

CALVIN COOLIDGE, *Governor.*"

"Given at the Executive Chamber, in Boston, this twenty-fourth day of September, in the year of our Lord one thousand nine hundred and nineteen, and of the Independence of the United States of America the one hundred and forty-fourth.

CALVIN COOLIDGE.

By His Excellency the Governor:
HERBERT H. BOYNTON,
*Deputy, Acting Secretary
of the Commonwealth.*

God save the Commonwealth of Massachusetts."

ON HUMANITY

[Copy]

The White House
Washington

My dear Mr. Lucey:

Not often do I see you or write you but I want you to know that if it were not for you I should not be here and I want to tell you how

much I love you. Do not work too much now
and try to enjoy yourself in your well-earned
hours of age.

Yours sincerely,

CALVIN COOLIDGE.

August 6, 1923.

[Mr. James Lucey is a cobbler at Northampton.]

ON LEGISLATION

Some attitudes on Beacon Hill. For anti-
monopoly bill. For injunction-modification bill.
For anti-discrimination bill. For direct sena-
torial elections. For woman's suffrage. For
honest small coal sales. For one day's rest in
seven. For improved working conditions,
women and children. For factory surgical
equipment. For pensions, widows and children
of firemen. For teachers' pensions. For play-
grounds. For low fares, workingmen and children. For full train crew bill. For improved
milk situation. For forty-eight-hour bill, women
and children. For eliminating profiteering in
rents. For preference to veterans. For employ-
ment for veterans. For revision of banking
laws.

CHAPTER XI

THE LESSON

"A youth, who bore, 'mid snow and ice,
A banner, with the strange device,
'Excelsior'."

IT is not the first hope of His First Biography simply to amuse nor even simply to interest. An hour of laughter, only, is an hour lost except as it implies necessary relaxation and recuperation for serious progress. His First Biography is a lesson, a hope to stimulate.

The first ambition of all the earth is happiness, its best ambition and its easiest ambition when founded, not on the hope of getting but on the power of giving. A motor sweeps up Beacon Street with the aristocratic purr of the Pierce, passing some one struggling towards the city on his feet. He, in his turn, is indifferent to the car, to wealth and to its display, to money and to what it will buy. His hopes do not lead him that way. His aspirations are not fixed on kennels and racing stables, deer parks and houses

148

12	PRESIDENT, 1923
11	VICE-PRESIDENT, 1921–23
10	GOVERNOR, 1919–20
9	LIEUTENANT-GOVERNOR, 1916–18
8	PRESIDENT OF STATE SENATE, 1914–15
7	STATE SENATOR, 1912–15
6	MAYOR, 1910–11
5	STATE REPRESENTATIVE, 1907–8
4	CHAIRMAN — CITY COMMITTEE, 1904
3	CLERK OF COURTS, 1903
2	CITY SOLICITOR, 1900-1
1	COUNCILMAN, 1899

HIS POLITICAL LADDER

and lands. He is not only indifferent, he is content, for he knows that happiness can not be
bought in that way. More than this, he is happy
and almost proud, not for what he has not,
material possessions, but for what he can do, for
he can write a great poem, paint a great picture
or control a great audience. Likewise, Calvin
Coolidge has found happiness, not in what he
has had but in the day's work, in what he has
done, in the development of the science of government for the advancement of the cause of
civilization.

The story of Calvin Coolidge is an amazing
story, none more so. A red-haired, freckled boy
on a plain farm, who was not a leader even
among the boys of a small Vermont village, has
become President of the United States. He
always kept on going, from the farm, on the
farm, up and on and always. He has become a
second "rail-splitter." Like Niagara, his is a
story which grows on one, and, as it is studied,
it overwhelms. And yet, while Roosevelt was a
torrent, Coolidge is a steady stream. His is a
story for every father and mother and child, a
story of responsibilities for the first, and of
opportunity for the last.

The story of Calvin Coolidge is a lesson for every American and for those across the seas, of hope and realization; that America is a country of law, order and opportunity; that success and happiness come to one, not because of what is around him, family, fashion and fortune, but because of what is in him, not for what he has, but for what he is; and that there is no end to the path upwards when uncommon sense, fidelity, preparation and Providence walk hand in hand.

His First Biography is a short lesson. It is a strong lesson. It is a stimulating lesson. It symbolizes the force of those great words of the Scriptures:

"Thou hast been faithful over a few things.
I will make thee ruler over many."

THE END.